Hong Kong Area by Area

Streetsmart

The information in this DK Eyewitness
Top 10 Travel Guide is checked regularly.
Every effort has been made to ensure that
this book is as up-to-date as possible at the
time of going to press. Some details,
however, such as telephone numbers,
opening hours, prices, gallery hanging
arrangements and travel information are
liable to change. The publishers cannot
accept responsibility for any consequences
arising from the use of this book, nor for any
material on third party websites, and cannot

Within each Top 10 list in this book, no hierarc'
of quality or popularity is implied. All 10 are, i
the editor's opinion, of roughly equal merit.

Front cover and spine *The stunning Hong
Kong skyline at night*
Back cover *Junk boat in Victoria Harbour*
Title page *The impressive Chi Lin Nunnery,
a Buddhist temple on Diamond Hill, Kowloc*

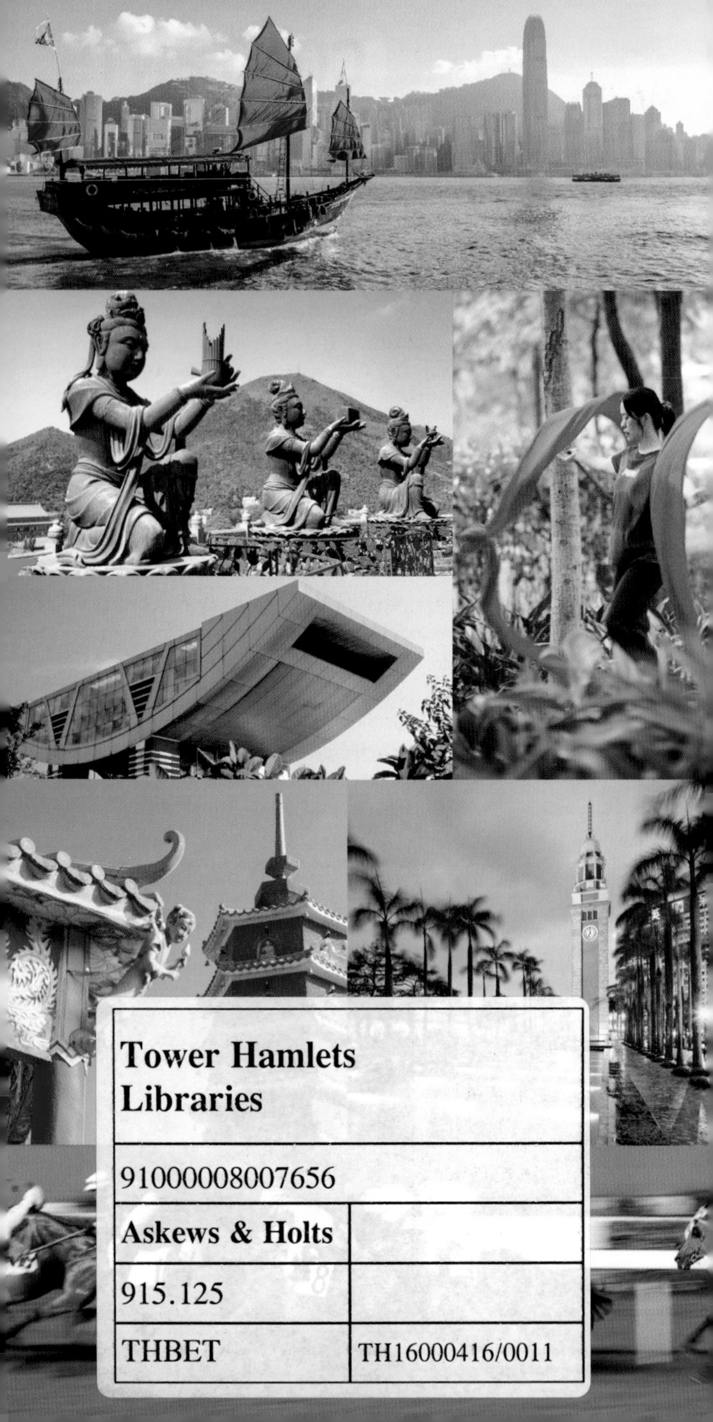

Welcome to
Hong Kong

Financial hub. Former colonial trophy. Showcase for avant-garde architecture. Shopping mecca. Melting pot of cultures. Hong Kong is all these things and more... so who could argue when we say it's Asia's most exciting territory? With Eyewitness Top 10 Hong Kong, it's yours to explore.

We love Hong Kong: the seething crowds, the futuristic harbourside cityscapes, the unashamed lust for success. What could be better than shopping for designer fashion in **Tsim Sha Tsui**'s malls, looking down over the frenetic city from the cool heights of the **Peak**, riding the romantic **Star Ferry** between Kowloon and Hong Kong Island, breakfasting on Michelin-starred **dim sum** or joining the cheering crowds for a night at the **Happy Valley horse races**? It's all here, packed into this tiny territory on China's Pearl River Delta.

Yet Hong Kong isn't all just superficial glitz. Along with the neighbouring cities of **Macau**, **Shenzhen** and **Guangzhou**, there are centuries of history here; the population is a melange of Chinese, European, Indian and southeast Asian migrants. Glimpse the different cultures inside smoky temples, at dawn tai chi sessions in the parks, in traditional **New Territory** villages, or amongst the bustling market stalls. The packed calendar of events offers a similar mix, from the annual **Rugby Sevens** to the ear-shattering firework displays that ring in the **Chinese New Year**.

This guide is designed to bring together the best of everything the territory has to offer, from **Tai Long Wan**'s best beaches to the hottest nightclubs in **Lan Kwai Fong**. There are tips throughout, plus 11 easy-to-follow itineraries, designed to tie together a clutch of sights in a short space of time. Add inspiring photography and detailed maps, and you have the essential pocket-sized travel companion. **Enjoy the book, and enjoy Hong Kong.**

Clockwise from top: **Junk boat in Victoria Harbour, tai chi practice, Clock Tower in Kowloon, Happy Valley Races, Ten Thousand Buddhas Monastery, Peak Tower, Po Lin Monastery**

Exploring Hong Kong

For the sheer variety of things to see and do, visitors to Hong Kong are spoiled for choice. Whether you are here for a short stay or just wanting a flavour of this great city, you need to make the most of your time. From jaw-dropping cityscape views to remote tropical beaches, here are some ideas for two and four days of sightseeing in Hong Kong.

Man Mo Temple is dedicated to the gods of war and literature.

The Peak Tram provides its passengers with some of the best views of Central's skyscrapers as it climbs to the top.

Ngong Ping 360 cable car

Lantau Island

Macau (40 km)

Big Buddha *Po Lin Monastery*

Mui Wo

Two Days in Hong Kong

Day ❶
MORNING
Begin on Hong Kong Island with a dim sum breakfast, then follow Hollywood Road to the **Man Mo Temple** (see p67). Continue to **Statue Square** (see pp14–15) to admire the modern architecture.
AFTERNOON
Head to **Stanley village** (see pp20–21) for low-key beaches and dinner. Ascend the **Peak** (see pp12–13) for city views during the Symphony of Lights (8pm daily), before downing a nightcap at **Lan Kwai Fong** (see p66).

Day ❷
MORNING
Catch an early ferry to Lantau Island and ride on the Ngong Ping 360

cable car to the **Big Buddha, Po Lin Monastery** (see pp32–3).
AFTERNOON
Head to **Kowloon Park** (see p87) to people-watch, or on Sundays to see a martial art display at its Kung Fu Corner (2:30–4:30pm). After shopping along **Nathan Road** (see p85), wander Temple Street Night Market for a souvenir and some alfresco dining at a *dai pai dong* (see pp22–3). Round off the evening with a cocktail at swanky **Felix Bar** (see p52).

Four Days in Hong Kong

Day ❶
MORNING
Ascend the Peak for glorious views of the city and its islands, and glimpse some of the world's most expensive properties (see pp12–13).

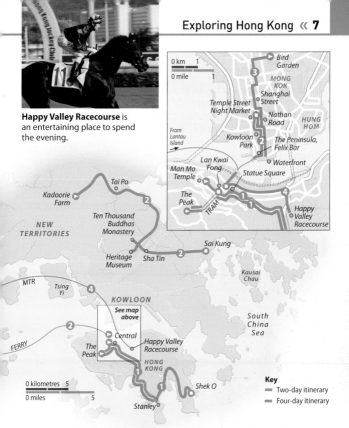

Happy Valley Racecourse is an entertaining place to spend the evening.

AFTERNOON
Check out **Hollywood Road** and **Man Mo Temple** (see p67) before crossing south to **Stanley** (see pp20–21). End the day with an evening meal here or at beachside **Shek O village** (see p81).

Day ❷
MORNING
Spend the whole morning at **Kadoorie Farm** (see p108).
AFTERNOON
After lunch from **Tai Po's markets** (see p112) spend a few hours at the **Heritage Museum** (see pp26–7) and **Ten Thousand Buddhas Monastery** (see p107), before heading to **Sai Kung** for a seafood meal (see p110).

Day ❸
MORNING
Begin the day at the **Bird Garden** (see p59), then wind south through

Kowloon's fascinating markets to traditional stores along **Shanghai Street** (see p95).
AFTERNOON
Explore Nathan Road's shops, taking afternoon tea at the **Peninsula Hotel** (see p85). Watch the Symphony of Lights from the **Waterfront** (see p88), then head back to **Temple Street Night Market** to pick up some souvenirs, as well as food for dinner (see pp22–3).

Day ❹
ALL DAY
Spend a full day either exploring **Lantau Island** (see pp116–121) or gambling in the casinos of **Macau** (see pp122–9), and the evening at **Happy Valley**'s racetrack (see pp16–17). Celebrate a win or drown your sorrows afterwards at one of **Lan Kwai Fong**'s lively bars (see p66).

Top 10 Hong Kong Highlights

Big Buddha and Po Lin Monastery, Lantau Island

TOP 10 Hong Kong Highlights

From opium port to Cold War enclave to frenetic financial capital, Hong Kong has never been boring. East meets West in high style here, and the results amaze and delight. Prepare to experience one of the world's most dramatic urban environments.

1 The Peak
Take the tram to the lofty heights of Victoria Peak for an amazing view of the city skyline *(see pp12–13)*.

2 Central's Statue Square
Hong Kong Island's northwest is the region's administrative centre. Colonial remnants and modern architecture stand side by side on Statue Square *(see pp14–15)*.

Mai Po

Yuen Long

Ngar Hom Sha

Pat Heung

Pak Long

Lam Tei

Ma On Kong

NEW

Tuen Mun

Tai Lam Chung Reservoir

So Kwun Tan

Tsuen Wan

Chek Lap Kok ✈

Discovery Bay

Tung Chung

10

Lantau Island

Mui Wo

West Lamma Channel

Tong Fuk

0 km 5
0 miles 5

9

Cheung Chau Island

3 Happy Valley Races
Horse racing below the high-rises: Happy Valley racecourse is where Hong Kongers come to play *(see pp16–17)*.

4 Star Ferry
Ignore the subterranean road and rail links between Hong Kong Island and Kowloon. The thrilling way to cross the water is on the Star Ferry *(see pp18–19)*.

Stanley 5

An old fort steeped in colonial history and reminders of World War II, Stanley is a peaceful diversion from the frenetic city *(see pp20–21)*.

6 Temple Street Night Market

Kowloon is at its most atmospheric at night. Head up the peninsula to the narrow lanes of Yau Ma Tei for serious haggling *(see pp22–3)*.

7 Heritage Museum

Near Sha Tin in the New Territories, Hong Kong's best museum is a must. Splendid high-tech audiovisual displays cover the region's diverse cultural heritage and natural history *(see pp26–7)*.

Tai Long 8 Wan Coastline

The remote, rugged Sai Kung Peninsula in the New Territories is the place to find Hong Kong's finest beaches *(see pp28–9)*.

Cheung Chau 9 Island

Of the many islands around Hong Kong, tiny Cheung Chau is arguably the loveliest, with traces of old China *(see pp30–31)*.

10 Big Buddha and Po Lin Monastery

Visible from miles away, the Big Buddha is a major tourist destination *(see pp32–3)*.

TOP10 ⭐ **The Peak**

With Hong Kong's most scenic views, cooler climes and quiet wooded walks, it's no wonder Victoria Peak is so popular, in particular with tourists and the super rich, who occupy the exclusive properties clinging to its slopes. The Peak Tram takes under 10 minutes to reach Victoria Gap, pinning you to your seat as it's hauled up the sheer slope at the end of a single cable (don't worry, its safety record is spotless).

1 Peak Tower

The Peak Tram empties into an anvil-shaped mall **(above)** that houses shops, restaurants and the Sky Terrace 428 viewing gallery. Standing at 428 m (1,404 ft), this is the highest viewing platform in a city full of vertiginous observation points. The commercial emphasis may grate, but children will enjoy Madame Tussaud's waxworks.

2 World's Most Expensive Street

Pollock's Path, on the Peak, earned this title in 2013, in part thanks to 10 Skyhigh, the most expensive residential property ever sold in Hong Kong – for a record amount of $800 million.

3 Galleria

Although the imposing Peak Tower mall is hardly sensitive to its grand setting, there is a good range of places to eat and drink inside its Galleria, with great views down onto the city and harbour, and across to Lamma Island.

4 Barker and Plantation Roads

These usually quiet (although pavement-free) roads are worth wandering for a peep at some of the Peak's more expensive properties, including 23 Severn Road. Most of them have amazing harbour views. But dream on. You would have to be a millionaire just to afford a two-bedroom flat here.

5 The Peak Lookout

This much-loved, upmarket drinking and dining spot boasts a fine terrace, great food, an excellent wine list and friendly ambience.

6 Pok Fu Lam Country Park

For a gentle half-hour ramble, head down Pok Fu Lam Reservoir Road, then catch a bus back into town **(below)**.

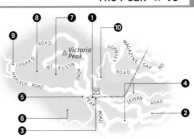

7 Victoria Peak Garden

The steep struggle up Mount Austin Road to these gardens is worth the effort. The viewing platform looks across the channel to Lamma Island **(left)**.

8 View near Summit

The summit itself is fenced off and covered by telecom masts, but the views from the edges of Victoria Peak Garden are excellent.

THE PEAK TRAM

Despite the fact that a single steel cable hauls the tram up a long and incredibly steep track, the Peak Tram has had a faultless safety record since the service opened in 1888. The most severe disruption to services came in the 1960s when torrents of water from an especially violent storm washed away part of the track.

NEED TO KNOW

MAP E5 ■ Peak Tram 7am–midnight daily

Single/return HK$28/$40 Bus 15C from Central Star Ferry ■ 2522 0922

www.thepeak.com.hk

■ If the weather is misty or there's low cloud, put off a visit to the Peak as you'll be able to see little of the excellent views.

■ Avoid taking the tram on weekends and public holidays as the queues are extremely long.

■ In the Peak Tower, Café Deco's wide food choices and good service make it a great drinking and dining stop. For the fantastic sea views over to Lamma Island, dine or have a drink on the Peak Lookout's lovely garden terrace.

9 Lugard and Harlech Roads

The effortless way to see most of the best views on offer from the Peak is on the shaded, well-paved, 3 km (2 mile) circular walk along Lugard Road and Harlech Road. It also makes for a terrific jogging track with a tremendous view **(above)**.

10 Old Peak Road

This former footpath up the Peak, created before the Peak Tram arrived, is pleasant and shaded. Surfaced, but incredibly steep, it is best saved for a descent. Take a detour onto Tregunter Path near the bottom to avoid the traffic.

TOP 10 ⭐ Central's Statue Square

Stand in Central district's Statue Square and you're right in the region's financial, political, historical and social heart. Among the steel and glass of the sleek modern skyscrapers surrounding the square are a few colonial remnants, including the handsome Neo-Classical Court of Final Appeal, outside which Hong Kong's usually low-key political demos take place. Shopping, which is a much more popular Hong Kong pursuit than politics, is enjoyed in the numerous swanky boutiques opposite.

Chater Garden ③
Despite the prime real-estate value of its site – on what was once the pitch of the Hong Kong Cricket Club – the small but well-tended Chater Garden **(right)** sprang up instead of a skyscraper. It's free to enter and makes a good place to enjoy a cold drink and rest tired legs.

① **Bank of China Tower**
Looming over the HSBC building is the imposing, 70-storey Bank of China Tower **(above)**. Renowned architect I M Pei designed the dizzying 367-m- (1,205-ft-) high tower. It doesn't please everyone – those who know about feng shui say it projects negative vibes onto other buildings.

② **Thomas Jackson Statue**
Appropriately, one of Hong Kong's few remaining statues, of a 19th-century HSBC banker **(right)**, is in Statue Square. The Japanese army removed one of Queen Victoria, which gave the square its name.

④ **The Cenotaph**
Standing at the northern edge of Statue Square, the Cenotaph is a memorial to those who died in the two world wars.

⑤ **Shopping Malls**
Two of Hong Kong's most up-market shopping malls – the busy Landmark Centre and the less busy Prince's Building (see p69) – sit next to Statue Square. They are home to many exclusive and elegant boutiques, including Armani, Gucci and Prada.

NEED TO KNOW
MAP L5

■ For a terrific bird's-eye view over Central and the harbour, head to the viewing gallery on the 43rd floor of the Bank of China Tower. Alternatively, try the wraparound terrace at Sevva Bar and Restaurant (see p70).

■ If you fancy picnicking in the square or in nearby Chater Garden, try the fantastic pastries, cakes and quiches from the Mandarin Oriental's Cake Shop, which is at the edge of the square.

6 Mandarin Oriental
At only 91 m (298 ft), it's hard to believe, but the Mandarin Oriental was once Hong Kong's tallest building. Today its graceful exterior seems overwhelmed by the ceaseless traffic, but inside it's still one of Hong Kong's finest hotels.

SUFFOCATING SUFFRAGE

During Handover negotiations *(see p37)*, China was adamant that Hong Kong's Legislative Council would be as democratic under Chinese rule as under the British (in other words, it could be argued, hardly at all). When Chris Patten, the last governor, tried introducing greater representation, China dubbed him "a serpent" among other things.

8 Former French Mission
Behind the HSBC building, this handsome mid-19th-century red-brick edifice has served as a French Catholic mission, Hong Kong's first Government House and, until 2015, the Court of Final Appeal.

7 HSBC Bank Headquarters
On its completion in 1985, Norman Foster's bold building was the most expensive ever built, costing more than HK$5bn. The edifice is said to have the strongest feng shui in Hong Kong. Rubbing the paws of the bank's handsome lions is said to bring good luck.

9 Sunday Filipino Fiesta
Hundreds of young Indonesians and Filipinos, mostly domestic workers enjoying their only day off, occupy almost every spare bit of public space throughout Central.

10 Court of Final Appeal
This Neo-Classical building **(above)** – a rare survivor from the city's colonial period – housed the Legislative Council, Hong Kong's equivalent to a parliament. The Court of Final Appeal moved here in 2015.

TOP 10 ⭐ Happy Valley Races

Feel the earth move beneath thundering hooves as you cheer the finishers home in the ultimate Hong Kong night out. Races have been held at Happy Valley – the widest stretch of flat land on Hong Kong Island, originally a swamp – since 1846. Today, the action takes place beneath twinkling high-rises, making for one of the most atmospheric horse-racing tracks in the world.

1 Wednesday Night Races
The most exciting scheduled races are usually on Wednesday evenings **(below)**. For the full atmosphere, jump on a Happy Valley-bound tram and bone up on the form in the Wednesday *Racing Post* on the way. Races are from 7:15pm to 11pm.

Happy Valley Racecourse

2 Happy Wednesday
With its many bars and restaurants, Wednesday nights here have become popular for mid-week partying. Entertainment includes live music, DJs and street performers.

HONG KONG'S BIGGEST PAYOUT

A then world-record total of US$92m was paid out at Happy Valley's sister track, Sha Tin, in 1997. Over 350 bets of HK$10 each collected HK$2 million.

3 Racing Museum
The small and neat museum **(below)** details Hong Kong's racing history and has a selection of art. Learn the story of the old trade in prized Mongolian and Chinese ponies. It is closed during race meetings.

4 View from Moon Koon
For a fantastic track-side view, go to Moon Koon Restaurant. Racing and dining packages are available.

5 Come Horseracing Tour
Splendid Tours and Grey Line both run this tour during scheduled race meetings. Tours include entry to the Members' Enclosure, welcome drink, a buffet meal and guide service.

6 Silver Lining Skeleton

Silver Lining, Hong Kong's most famous horse, was the first to win more than HK$1 million. The equine skeleton takes pride of place in a glass cabinet at the Racing Museum.

8 The Crowd

Happy Valley has a 55,000 capacity **(above)**, but is so popular that it sometimes sells out before the day. The enthusiasm among the big-betting, chain-smoking punters is infectious. Stand in the open next to the track, for the best atmosphere.

9 Types of Bet

Ways to bet include guessing the winner; a place (picking 1st or 2nd, or 1st, 2nd or 3rd if seven or more horses race); a quinella (picking 1st and 2nd in any order); and a quinella place (any two of the first three horses).

10 Where to Bet

Bets are placed at the counters at the back of each floor of the main stand. If you win, wait for a few minutes after the race, then go to the same counter to collect your winnings.

7 Jockey Club Booths

For help and advice on placing bets go to the friendly Jockey Club officials **(below)** at the booths between the main entrance and the racetrack. The Jockey Club is the only organization allowed to take bets in Hong Kong. The tax it collects makes up a small but significant percentage of government revenue, but is being threatened by illegal and online betting.

NEED TO KNOW

MAP P6 ▪ Less than 1 km (0.5 miles) south of Causeway Bay on Hong Kong Island ▪ Meets Wed, and occasionally, Sat & Sun (Sep–Jul) ▪ Dial 1817 for race details ▪ www.hkjc.com ▪ www.happy valleyracecourse.com ▪ Adm HK$10 (standing); HK$20 (seated)

Racing Museum: 2966 8065; noon–7pm (to 9pm on race days)

Come Horseracing Tour: 2316 2151, call ahead for prices

▪ A Tourist Ticket, available with a passport at the Badge Inquiry Office, will give you access to the upper seats.

▪ Moon Koon Restaurant, on the second floor of the main stand, offers good, reasonably priced Chinese food. Advance booking is required on race nights (2966 7111 or online at www.hkjc.com).

🔟 ⭐ Star Ferry

One of Hong Kong's best-loved institutions, the Star Ferries have shuttled people between Kowloon and Hong Kong Island since 1888. They are still used by commuters despite the advent of rail and road tunnels beneath the harbour. A ferry ride offers a thrilling perspective on the towering skyscrapers and the jungle-clad hills of Hong Kong Island. Take an evening voyage for the harbour's daily neon spectacle, A Symphony of Lights, when 45 buildings on both sides of the harbour put on a light and sound show.

1 The Fleet
In the early days, four coal-fired boats went back and forth between Hong Kong and Kowloon. Today, 12 diesel-powered vessels operate, each named after a particular star (with the night-time glare and pollution, the only stars you're likely to see from the harbour).

2 Clock tower
Standing next to the Tsim Sha Tsui Star Ferry, the land-mark clock tower **(left)** is the last remnant of the old Kowloon railway terminus completed in 1915. This was the poetic final stop for trains from the mainland, including the Orient Express.

3 Star Ferry Crew
Many Star Ferry crew members still sport old-fashioned uniforms, making popular photo-graphic subjects. Watch out, too, for the crewmen catching the mooring rope with a long billhook.

4 Skyline South
As you cross Victoria Harbour from Kowloon, on the far left you'll see the glass and flowing lines of the Convention Centre **(above)** in Wan Chai and above it the 373-m (1,223-ft) tower of Central Plaza. Further right are the Bank of China's striking zig-zags, and the HSBC building. However, the real giant is Two IFC (see pp38–9), Hong Kong Island's tallest skyscraper.

9 Ocean Terminal
Just north of the Tsim Sha Tsui terminal, Hong Kong's cruise ships dock, including the world's most famous liners **(below)**. Some US warships also dock here during port calls.

5 Hong Kong Maritime Museum
Opened in 2013, this museum explores the vast maritime history and trade of the Pearl River Delta, from the Song Dynasty through to the present day, as well as the marine life of the South China Sea **(above)**.

NEED TO KNOW

MAP L4 ■ Ferries TST to Wan Chai 7:20am–11pm, TST to Central 6:30am–11:30pm

Ferry tours of the harbour: 2367 7065; www.starferry.com.hk

A Symphony of Lights: Every night at 8pm; www.tourism.gov.hk/symphony

Hong Kong Maritime Museum: Central Pier No. 8. 3713 2500; www.hkmaritime museum.org; 9:30am–5:30pm Mon–Fri, 10am–7pm Sat, Sun & public hols

■ The HKTB office in the Tsim Sha Tsui Star Ferry building is the most convenient place to pick up brochures, get help and advice, and buy Star Ferry models and other souvenirs.

6 Star Ferry Routes
The ferries operate daily between Tsim Sha Tsui and Central every 6 to 12 minutes, and between Tsim Sha Tsui and Wan Chai every 8 to 20 minutes.

7 Sightseeing Bargain
With fares ranging from just HK$2 to HK$3.40, a crossing on a Star Ferry is one of Hong Kong's best sightseeing bargains.

8 Tours
Star Ferries run several afternoon and evening ferry tours of the harbour on their "Shining Star" ferry, which is more comfortable than the regular ferry. The Shining Star ferry has an air-conditioned top deck as well as a café.

10 Skyline North
As you approach Kowloon **(below)**, you'll see the Arts and Cultural Centre closest to the shore. Behind it rises the grand extension of the Peninsula Hotel, with the huge ICC Tower gleaming to the west.

TOP 10 ⭐ Stanley

Originally a sleepy fishing haven, Stanley was the largest settlement on Hong Kong Island before the British moved in. The modern town, hugging the southern coast, still makes a peaceful, pleasant escape from the bustle of the city. Traffic is minimal, and the pace of life relaxed, with plenty of excellent places to eat, good beaches and a large market to search for cheap clothing, silks and souvenirs. Stanley is also the place to glimpse colonial Hong Kong and an older Chinese tradition seen at the Tin Hau Temple.

1 Market
Reasonably priced clothes, shoes and accessories as well as plenty of tourist tat are to be found among Stanley's pleasant, ramshackle market stalls **(above)**. Although it's not the cheapest or best market in Hong Kong, it's worth visiting before heading to one of the seafront eateries.

2 Old Police Station
The handsome structure was built in 1859 and is Hong Kong's oldest surviving police station. The Japanese used it as a headquarters during World War II. It is now a supermarket.

Hiking above Stanley

3 Murray House
Shifted here from its original site in Central to make way for the Bank of China Tower *(see p14)*, this 1843 Neo-Classical relic now houses several restaurants **(below)**. Adjacent Blake Pier is the departure point for ferries to remote Po Toi island *(see p119)*.

4 Waterfront
The pretty waterfront makes for a pleasant promenade between the market area and Murray House. The harbour was once home to a busy fleet of junks and fishing boats, but is now largely empty **(above)**.

⑤ Tin Hau Temple
This temple is one of the oldest in Hong Kong. Lined with the grimacing statues of guards to the sea goddess Tin Hau, the interior of this 1767 temple is also one of the most evocative **(above)**.

⑥ Stanley Beach
This fine stretch of sand is perfect for a dip and a paddle. It's the venue for the fiercely contested dragon boat races in June *(see p61)*.

⑦ War Cemetery
Most of the graves are the resting place of residents who died during World War II. Others date back to early colonial days, when many succumbed to tropical illnesses.

THE WAR DEAD
After Japan overran Hong Kong in 1941 *(see p80)*, captured civilians suffered for three years under a regime of neglect, starvation and torture. Many of those who died are buried at Stanley cemetery.

⑧ Stanley Fort
The old British army barracks at the end of the peninsula is now occupied by the Chinese People's Liberation Army (closed to the public).

⑨ St Stephen's Beach
Another good stretch of sand, St Stephen's is also the place to organize sailing and canoeing. Make use of the barbecue pits for an open-air lunch.

NEED TO KNOW
MAP F6 ■ Buses 6, 6A, 6X, 66 or 260 from Exchange Square, Central

Stanley market: www.hk-stanley-market.com; 9am–6pm daily

■ If you hate crowds, avoid Stanley at weekends when the town and market become very busy and the buses to and from Central fill up.

■ Sit at the front of the top deck of the bus to fully appreciate the dramatic coast road out to Stanley.

■ For alfresco dining, The Boathouse on Stanley's waterfront offers modern European and American cuisine and sea views from the balcony seating *(see p83)*.

⑩ Pubs and Restaurants
One of Stanley's best attractions is its excellent range of restaurants and bars *(see p83)*, including The Boathouse **(right)**. A host of eateries, from Italian to Vietnamese, line Stanley Main Road, facing the sea. Murray House also has good restaurants.

🔟 ⭐ Temple Street Night Market

Beneath the bleaching glare of a thousand naked light bulbs, tourists and locals alike pick their way among the stalls crowding the narrow lanes of Yau Ma Tei's Temple Street. The overwhelming array of cheap goods includes clothes, shoes, accessories, designer fakes, copy CDs, bric-a-brac and a generous helping of junk. Prices here may be a bit higher than in Shenzhen, just over the Chinese border, or in some of Hong Kong's less well-known markets, but Temple Street is unbeatable for atmosphere.

① Fortune Tellers
Fortune tellers operate around the junction of Temple and Market streets. Most are face and palm readers. The caged finches are trained to pick a fortune card from the pack in return for some seeds.

② Canto Opera Street Performers
On some evenings, musicians and singers perform popular Cantonese opera numbers next door to the fortune tellers **(below)**.

③ Dai Pai Dong
Tighter health regulations have made *dai pai dong* food stalls a rare sight, but they are alive and well at Temple Street, selling a variety of Chinese snacks **(below)**, savoury pancakes, fishballs, seafood kebabs and unspecified meat offerings.

Temple Street Night Market

④ Reclamation St Canteens
If you haven't had your fill from the *dai pai dong*, try the cheap noodles and rice dishes at the stalls on Reclamation Street. Don't mind your neighbour's table manners; it's customary to drop or spit gristle and bone onto the table-tops.

5 Best Watches

It's likely to be a decent timekeeper but with no guarantee. The local makes and Western fakes are usually good value for money **(left)**. One stall offers genuine secondhand watches.

6 Best Clothes

Amid the naff and poly-fabric horrors, good buys include cheap T-shirts, elaborate silks, beaded tops and cotton dresses **(right)**. Have a look at the stall on the corner of Kansu Street.

7 Best Leather Goods

Leather is not really Temple Street's strong point. But belts are cheap, and there are plenty of leather handbags and shoulder bags, including fake Gucci, Elle and Burberry items. Some are more convincing than others.

HAGGLING

Remember, prices given are mostly starting points and the mark-ups are significant. The merchandise here is far cheaper than in China, so haggle hard (but do it with a smile), and remember the vendor is making a profit whatever price you both agree on. Begin below half the asking price and you should be able to get 50 per cent off most items.

8 Best Shoes

From the very cheap flip-flops to the reasonable suede or leather shoes, bargain footwear is available almost everywhere on Temple Street, although the variety is not huge and the styles not that elegant. A few stalls sell designer fakes.

10 Best Knick-knacks

Mao memorabilia, old posters, coins, opium pipes and jade are found on Public Square Street. Temple Street's north end is rich in kitsch plastic Japanese cartoon merchandise, including Afro Ken and Pokémon, and lucky *maneki-neko* cat figurines **(right)**.

9 Best Accessories

Cheap sunglasses **(below)** are easy to find. Embroidered and beaded handbags and shoulder bags are also worth looking out for.

NEED TO KNOW

MAP M1–2 ▪ The market opens at 4pm, but really gets going after 7pm and goes on until as late as midnight.

▪ A good way to tackle the night market is to start at the top by taking the MTR to Yau Ma Tei (Exit C) and walk south from Portland Street. This way you'll end up closer to the restaurants, hotels and bars of Tsim Sha Tsui when you've finished shopping.

▪ Buy a snack from the *dai pai dong* (street food stalls).

TOP 10 ⭐ Heritage Museum

This modern museum, on the outskirts of Sha Tin in the New Territories, is one of Hong Kong's best. Opened in 2000, the Hong Kong Heritage Museum has six permanent galleries and six changing galleries covering the culture, arts and natural history of Hong Kong and the New Territories. Exciting audiovisual exhibits, a range of temporary exhibitions and a good interactive children's section make for a fun day out for visitors of all ages.

Architecture and Design ①

The Heritage Museum building **(right)** is based on the traditional Chinese *si he yuan* style, built around a courtyard. The style is still visible in the villages of the New Territories *(see p110)*.

② Orientation Theatre

For a brief overview of the museum, visit the Orientation Theatre on the ground floor opposite the ticket office.

③ Children's Discovery Gallery

The brightly coloured gallery is a vibrant, fun way to introduce children to local nature and archaeology, and the history of toys. Interactive exhibits and the child-size 3-D models are very popular with young children **(left)**.

Cantonese Opera Heritage Hall ④

Cantonese opera is an obscure subject. However, the sumptuous costumes, intricate stage settings and snatches of song from the elaborate operas of Guangdong and Guangxi on display in this gallery go some way towards illustrating this popular attraction **(right)**.

NEED TO KNOW

MAP E3 ■ 1 Man Lam Road, Sha Tin, New Territories ■ 2180 8188 ■ www.heritagemuseum.gov.hk ■ MTR to Kowloon Tong, then bus 80M or MTR to Che Kung Temple, then a 5-minute walk

Open 10am–6pm Mon, Wed–Fri, 10am–7pm Sat, Sun & public hols

Adm: HK$10 (free on Wed)

■ Combine a visit to the museum with a trip to the races at Sha Tin if you can *(see p107)*.

■ There is a small café and gift shop in the lobby.

Previous pages Central's skyscrapers from the Peak

Key to Floorplan
- Ground floor
- First floor
- Second floor

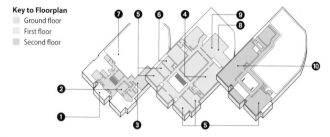

5 Thematic Exhibitions

Five halls on the first and second floors house temporary exhibitions focusing on subjects varying from popular culture, contemporary art and social issues in Hong Kong, to traditional Chinese art and history.

6 Chao Shao-an Gallery

The delicate ink on scroll paintings of artist and one-time Hong Kong resident Chao Shao-an are known far beyond China. There are dozens of fine examples on show in the gallery.

7 Courtyard

For fresh air and interesting surroundings, head to the shaded courtyard **(left)** in the centre of the complex.

9 New Territories Culture

Large mock-ups of old maritime and village scenes **(above)** recreate the pre-colonial days. The growth of the new towns, such as Sha Tin, is also covered through photography and objects.

10 TT Tsui Gallery of Chinese Art

The works of art dating from Neolithic times to the 20th century include porcelain, bronze, jade and stone artifacts, furniture, laquerware and religious statues **(below)**.

8 New Territories History

Examples of the rich fauna and flora of the region, along with 6,000-year-old artifacts from the early days of human habitation in Hong Kong, chart both the natural and social changes of the region.

HONG KONG'S EARLIEST SETTLERS

The New Territories History hall tells the scant story of Hong Kong's original inhabitants. Bronze Age people left behind axe and arrowheads in various parts of the territory more than 4,000 years ago, along with some mysterious rock carvings. Excavations on Lamma Island have turned up artifacts from an older Stone Age civilization, dating back about 6,000 years.

TOP 10 ⭐ Tai Long Wan Coastline

Although only 40 km (25 miles) from Hong Kong Island, the remote, pristine beaches on the eastern edge of the rugged Sai Kung Peninsula, in the New Territories, seem like another country. There is no rail link and few roads, so you will have to make an early start, taking a bus to Sai Kung town, another bus to Pak Tam Au, then walk the hilly 6-km (4-mile) footpath to the beach. Alternatively, hire a junk. The reward for your efforts will be stunning coastline, glorious surf, delightful hidden pools and shaded cafés.

1 Beaches
There are three excellent beaches at Tai Long Wan (above). Tai Wan is the most remote and unspoiled; the smallest beach, Ham Tin, has a good café and camping area; Tai Long Sai Wan is the busiest.

4 Ham Tin to Tai Long Path
Take the steep 1-km (half-mile) path between Ham Tin and Tai Long Sai Wan for lovely views down onto Ham Tin, Tai Wan and the mountains behind (below).

2 Natural Swimming Pools
A lovely series of waterfalls and natural swimming pools (left) is the area's best-kept secret. Reach them from the path running alongside the small river at the northwestern end of Tai Long Sai Wan beach.

3 Beach Cafés
Noodles, fried rice and hot and cold drinks are available from the modest, reasonably priced cafés on Tai Long Sai Wan and the Hoi Fung café at Ham Tin.

5 Surf Action
Tai Wan has reasonably good surf **(above)**. Bodyboarding should always be possible, and you may even be able to surf properly when storms raise bigger swells.

6 Pleasure Junks
Most privately hired junks drop anchor at Tai Long Sai Wan, and their passengers head to the beach in smaller craft, making this the busiest of the three beaches.

THE ROUTE OUT

A good route out of Tai Long Wan is the scenic path winding southwest from Sai Wan village around High Island Reservoir. Once you hit the main road outside Pak Tam Chung, there's a chance of picking up a bus or taxi back into Sai Kung town – but allow up to 5 hours walking just in case.

7 Hakka Fisherfolk
Tai Long village **(below)** may have been first settled in prehistoric times. It was a thriving Hakka fishing village until the 1950s, when most people migrated to the city or abroad. Only a few elderly residents remain in this sleepy place.

8 Camp Site
The area just east of Ham Tin village is the best place for overnight campers; it has flat ground, barbecue pits, public toilets and a stream for fresh water. There are no hotels in the area.

9 Sharp Peak
The prominent 468-m (1,497-ft) summit of Sharp Peak is clearly visible from Ham Tin and Tai Wan. The arduous climb up its very steep slopes rewards with spectacular views over the peninsula.

10 Ham Tin Bridge
If you want to keep your feet dry, the only way onto the beach from Ham Tin village is via a rickety bridge. Marvel at the makeshift engineering from nailed-together driftwood and offcuts **(right)**.

NEED TO KNOW

MAP H3 ■ Take the frequent 92 bus from Diamond Hill KCR terminating at Sai Kung town, then the half-hourly 94 bus (or 96R on Sun) to Pak Tam Au. Allow about 90 minutes from Kowloon or Central to the start of the path, plus at least an hour each way to hike to and from the beach

Daily junk hire from HK$5,500; see *Yellow Pages* for listings

■ Buy the HKTB's *Discover Hong Kong's Nature* for detailed information.

■ The only eating options are beach cafés, or you can stock up for a picnic at Sai Kung town.

■ For supplies, head to the well-stocked Wellcome supermarket in Sai Kung.

TOP 10 ⭐ Cheung Chau Island

This tiny, charming island, a half-hour high-speed ferry ride west of Hong Kong, makes a great escape from the heat and hassles of the city, except maybe at weekends when everyone else has the same idea. The sense of an older, traditional Hong Kong is pervasive among the narrow streets, tiny shops and temples of this old pirate and fishing haven. It's possible to see most of the island in a day, taking it in with some lovely secluded walks. The seafood is cheap and there are small but excellent stretches of beach.

Pak Tai Temple ①
This highly decorative, renovated 1783 temple **(right)** is dedicated to Pak Tai, Cheung Chau's patron deity, who is credited with saving islanders from plague. The temple is the centre for the annual Bun Festival celebrations *(see p60)*, when mounds of buns are piled up to be offered to resident ghosts. The festival dates from the time of plagues in the 19th century, which were considered to be the vengeance of those killed by local pirates.

② Harbour
Although Hong Kong's commerical fishing industry has dwindled from its heyday, plenty of fishing boats still operate from Cheung Chau's typhoon shelter harbour **(above)**. Cheap cycle hire is available along the waterfront.

③ Venerable Banyan Tree
On Tung Wan Road is an ancient tree **(below)** that is thought to be the source of Cheung Chau's good fortune. It is so revered by islanders that a restaurant opposite was knocked down instead of the tree to make way for a road.

PATHS AND WALKS

A footpath weaves around the southern edge of the island, taking in clifftop walks and a small Tin Hau Temple at Moring Beach. Heading southwest will take you along Peak Road past the cemetery to Sai Wan harbour. From here you can take a sampan shuttle back to the ferry pier.

④ Windsurfing Centre
The family of Olympic gold medallist Lee Lai-Shan operates the windsurfing centre and café near Tung Wan.

5 Tung Wan Beach
The island's finest beach **(above)** is on the east coast, 150 m (500 ft) from the west coast's ferry pier. It is tended by lifeguards and has a shark net.

6 "The Peak"
A walk up the hill along Don Bosco and Peak roads will take you past some lovely old colonial houses and beautiful sea views. The cemetery on Peak Road has especially fine vistas.

7 Pirate's Cave
The place where 19th-century buccaneer Cheung Po-tsai supposedly stashed his booty, this "cave" is more of a hole or crevice **(right)**. Take a torch to explore. The sea views nearby make it worth the trip.

8 Boatbuilding Yard
At the harbour's northern end is a busy yard where junks are built and nets mended. Look out for the slabs of ice sliding along the overhead chute, down a mini helter-skelter and onto the boats.

9 Seafood Restaurants
If you want to dine on fish or shellfish, there's plenty of choice along the seafront on She Praya Road north and south of the ferry pier. The restaurants are cheaper than other seafood centres such as Lamma. Choose from the live tanks.

NEED TO KNOW

MAP C6 ■ Daily ferries hourly or half-hourly from Central Pier No. 5. High-speed ferries take just 35 minutes
■ www.hkkf.com.hk

■ Hire bicycles from opposite the basketball courts close to Pak Tai Temple.

■ Cheung Chau's famous Bun Festival is held in early May, check www.hktb.com for dates.

■ If you've had your fill of seafood, try Morocco's (2986 9767), by the ferry pier, which serves decent Indian, Thai and Western (but not Moroccan) fare in the evenings.

10 Ancient Rock Carving
In the Hong Kong region are several rock carvings in close proximity to the sea. There are some near Tung Wan beach and Cheung Chau has one facing the sea. Nothing is known of the people who carved out these shapes about 3,000 years ago **(left)**.

TOP 10 ⭐ Big Buddha and Po Lin Monastery

Once a humble house built in 1906 by three monks to worship the Buddha, Po Lin Monastery on Lantau Island is now a large and important temple. Its crowning glory, the giant Buddha statue facing the monastery, is an object of veneration for devotees and one of Hong Kong's most popular tourist sights. The statue dominates the area from a plinth reached by more than 260 steps. On a clear day, the view across the valleys, reservoirs and peaks of Lantau makes the climb more than worthwhile.

The Big Buddha (1)

Standing a lofty 34-m (112-ft) high, this mighty bronze statue **(right)** is among the largest seated Buddha images in the world. The statue, which was cast in more than 220 pieces, sits on a lotus throne – the Buddhist symbol of purity – and his right hand is raised, "imparting fearlessness".

(2) Monastery

Attracted by its seclusion in Lantau's hills, Buddhist monks began arriving on Lantau in the early 20th century. The Po Lin or "precious lotus" monastery really developed as a place for pilgrimage in the 1920s when the Great Hall was built and the first abbot appointed **(below)**.

(4) Ngong Ping 360 Cable Car

The cable-car ride from Tung Chung to Po Lin is an attraction in itself **(below)**. The 4-mile (5.7-km), 25-minute journey provides sweeping views across the North Lantau Country Park and to the distant South China Sea (see p49).

(3) Tea Gardens

Just west of the Buddha, the gardens boast their own modest tea plantation. The café sells the tea leaves and makes a pleasant place to enjoy a drink or meal.

5 Great Hall

The main temple houses three large golden Buddha images **(above)**. Don't miss the ceiling paintings, the elaborate exterior friezes and the elegant lotus-shaped floor tiles.

8 Footpath Down to Tung Chung

Walk down to Tung Chung MTR via the lovely 4-mile (7-km) wooded path through the Tung Chung Valley. You'll pass smaller monasteries including Lo Hon, which serves vegetarian lunches.

9 Monks and Nuns

You may glimpse the robed, shaven-headed nuns and monks at prayer in the old temple behind the main one. Entry is forbidden to tourists during the 3pm prayers.

10 Temple Gateway

Guarded by twin lions, the temple gateway **(below)** is said to replicate the southern gate to Buddhist heaven. As found elsewhere in the temple, it is decorated with reverse

swastikas, which is the holy sign of Buddhism. The Chinese characters at the top read "Po Lin Monastery".

Bodhisattvas 6

On each side of the staircase are statues of Buddhist saints **(right)**. They are venerated for deferring heaven in order to help mortals reach enlightenment.

7 Relic Inside the Buddha

A sacred relic of the real Buddha (a tooth in a crystal container) is enshrined within the Buddha image, but is difficult to make out. Below the statue is a display about the life of the Buddha and his path to enlightenment.

The Top 10 of Everything

A traditional Chinese dragon used
in ceremonial dances

🔟 Moments in History

1 **4000 BC: Early Peoples**
For many years, the popular version of history was that Hong Kong was a "barren rock" devoid of people when the British arrived. In fact, archaeology now shows that scattered primitive clans had settled by the seaside on Hong Kong Island and the New Territories some six millennia ago. Their diet was not politically correct by today's standards: bone fragments show they liked to eat dolphin.

2 **AD 1127: Local Clans**
When marauding Mongols drove the Song dynasty emperor's family out of the imperial capital of Kaifeng, one princess escaped to the walled village of Kam Tin in the New Territories, where she married into the powerful Tang clan.

3 **1841: The British Take Hong Kong Island**
In a decisive move during the First Opium War (1839–42) between China and Britain, Captain Charles Elliot of the British Royal Navy landed on Hong Kong Island and planted the Union Jack flag on 25 January. The 8,000-odd locals seem to take it in their stride, but China and Britain continued to fight

19th-century pirate

over other Chinese trading cities. The 1842 Treaty of Nanking ceded Hong Kong Island to the British.

4 **1860: Land Claim**
The good times were rolling in Hong Kong, where the population had swollen to more than 86,000. The island was becoming cramped, however, and after a series of further skirmishes between Britain and China, the Kowloon Peninsula and Stonecutter's Island were ceded to Britain by the Convention of Beijing.

5 **1898: The 99-Year Lease**
Britain dug in, turning Hong Kong into a mighty fort. Lyemun at the eastern end of the island bristled with guns and the world's first wire-guided torpedo. Breathing space and water supplies were assured when, on 1 July, the 99-year lease of the New Territories was signed in Beijing.

6 **1941: Japanese Occupation**
Hong Kong had guns galore defending the sea, but the Japanese came by land. They had little trouble breaching the aptly named Gin Drinkers Line – a motley string of pillboxes. Hong Kong was surrendered two days before Christmas, beginning a brutal three-year occupation.

Japanese soldiers captured by the British, 1945

1950: Economic Miracle

The territory's economic miracle began to unfold, as incoming refugees from China provided an eager workforce, and British rule kept things on an even keel. Hong Kong's transformation into a manufacturing centre began.

The Handover ceremony, 1997

 1997: Handover

Following the 1984 Sino-British joint Declaration, when Deng Xiaoping promised to preserve Hong Kong's autonomy under "One Country, Two Systems", Britain handed Hong Kong back to China at midnight on 30 June 1997. The ceremony appeared an anticlimax after escalating political tensions.

 1998: Financial Crisis

Asia's economic "tigers" were humbled, as years of living on borrowed money finally took their toll. Hong Kong was not as badly hit as some countries, but the financial crisis took its toll nonetheless.

2014: Occupy Central Protests

Following widespread protests demanding electoral reform in 2014, China plans to offer universal suffrage to Hong Kong citizens in 2017 – but only to elect candidates approved by Beijing.

TOP 10 MOVERS AND SHAKERS

1 Jorge Alvares
In 1513, the Portuguese navigator Alvares becomes the first European to visit Hong Kong.

2 Cheung Po-tsai
The Lantau-based pirate king Cheung Po-tsai wreaks havoc, plundering international traders in 1810.

3 Lin Zexu
Commissioner Lin Zexu is appointed by China in 1839, with the task of ending the trade in imported opium.

4 Captain Charles Elliot
Flag-planter Captain Charles Elliot claims Hong Kong Island for Britain and Queen Victoria in 1841.

5 Sir Henry Pottinger
Pottinger becomes Hong Kong's first governor. He turns a blind eye to illicit shipments of opium.

6 Dr Sun Yat-sen
The reformer blasts China as "chaotic and corrupt" during a lecture at Hong Kong University in 1923. Economic boycott of the colony follows.

7 Rensuke Isogai
In 1941, the military commander begins his barbaric reign as Japan's wartime governor of Hong Kong.

8 Deng Xiaoping
The Chinese premier sticks to his principles during Handover talks with Margaret Thatcher in 1984.

9 Chris Patten
Lachrymose last governor Chris Patten waves goodbye to Hong Kong in 1997.

10 Tung Chee-hwa
The shipping magnate Tung Chee-hwa becomes the first Chief Executive of Hong Kong after the Handover.

Deng Xiaoping

🔟 Modern Buildings

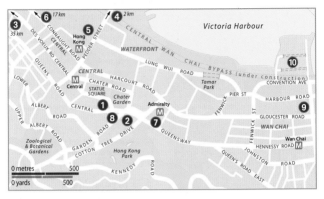

17 km

1 HSBC Headquarters
MAP L5 ▪ 1 Queen's Rd, Central

Sir Norman Foster's striking, Blade Runner-esque edifice cost a whopping HK$5.2bn, making it the world's priciest building when it opened in 1985. The headquarters of the Hong Kong and Shanghai Banking Corporation are reputed to have some of the best feng shui around – the building sits on a rare confluence of five "dragon lines" and enjoys unimpeded harbour views. The soaring atrium, filled with natural light, feels like a cathedral. Guarding the building's entrance are two lion statues named Stephen and Stitt.

HSBC Headquarters atrium

2 Bank of China Tower
MAP L6 ▪ 1 Garden Rd, Central ▪ 43/F viewing platform: open 9am–6pm Mon–Fri, 9am–1pm Sat

This one is also famous in feng shui circles, but more for dishing it out than possessing it – the glass-skinned tower shoots bad vibes at the old Government House and other colonial entities. Its knife-like edges were the inspiration of American-Chinese master architect I M Pei. The 70-storey, 367-m (1,205-ft) stack of prisms opened in 1990. Its viewing platform is the natural place to go for a sweeping city perspective.

3 Hong Kong International Airport
MAP B4

Another of Norman Foster's designs. His glass-dominated passenger terminal, which opened in July 1998, is impressive. The airport is built on the specially flattened island of Chek Lap Kok.

4 International Commerce Centre
MAP L2 ▪ 1 Austin Rd West, Kowloon

At 484 m (1,588 ft) in height and with 108 storeys, this is Hong Kong's tallest building. It houses the world's highest hotel, the Ritz-Carlton, Hong Kong (see p149) and the sky100 Observation Deck.

5 Two IFC Tower
MAP L5 ▪ Exchange Square, Central

The Two International Finance Centre Tower soars above Victoria

Two IFC Tower

Harbour. At 412 m (1,352 ft), it was Hong Kong's tallest building until it was overtaken in 2010 by the International Commerce Centre. There is a large, upmarket shopping mall at its base.

Tsing Ma Bridge
MAP D4

The suspension bridge stretches from Tsing Yi Island to Lantau, 2.2 km (1.5 miles) long. A striking sight, especially when lit up at night, the double-decker bridge carries both the road and rail links to Chek Lap Kok airport. It was opened in May 1997 by former UK Prime Minister Margaret Thatcher, having taken five years to build at a cost of HK$7.14bn. Take the MTR to Tsing Yi or catch an airport bus (but not the airport train) to view it. There's also a viewing platform at Ting Kau *(see p120)*.

Lippo Towers
MAP L–M6 ■ 89 Queensway, Admiralty

These knobbly megaliths look like they have koalas clinging to their sides – a reflection of the origins of the original antipodean owner, jailbird Alan Bond.

Cheung Kong Centre
MAP L6 ■ 2 Queen's Rd Central

This building is big, boxy and glassy. The top floor is the home of business magnate Li Ka-shing. Note how it's built perfectly parallel to the adjoining Bank of China for optimal feng shui.

Central Plaza
Confusingly, this is in Wan Chai, not Central *(see p73)*. The building has 78 storeys and at 374 m (1,227 ft) it is the third-tallest tower in Hong Kong. At night the neon rods at the top of the building change colour every 15 minutes.

Central Plaza

HK Convention and Exhibition Centre
MAP N5 ■ 1 Expo Drive, Wan Chai

Site of the official Handover ceremony in 1997, the Centre sprawls across a huge area over the harbour and was designed to resemble a bird in flight.

Tsing Ma Bridge at dusk from Tsing Yi island

🔟 Walking Routes and Promenades

Views of the skyscrapers of Central from the Peak Circuit

① The Peak Circuit

This loop around Victoria Peak takes about an hour to complete at a gentle pace. Formed by Harlech and Lugard roads, the circuit offers jaw-dropping city panoramas to the north, boundless sea views to the south, and glimpses of the many millionaires' homes among the greenery en route (see pp12–13).

② Temple Street Night Market

Allow plenty of time, not for the distance (Temple Street is no more than half a mile end to end), but to explore the pageantry of hawker stalls, fortune tellers, medicine men and opera singers that set up along here every night (see pp22–3).

③ The MacLehose Trail

MAP G3

It spans over 100 km (60 miles) across the New Territories, so only bona fide outdoor types will attempt the whole length. But certain sections are

easily accessible (try the lovely part around the High Island Reservoir) for visitors who value the prospect of being back at the hotel bar by nightfall. Information can be found on the HKTB website (see p145).

④ Central to Western via Hollywood Road

Central's futuristic office towers and concrete canyons give way to the low-rise charm of antique shops, galleries and bars the further west you go, ending up in Western's archetypal Chinese shopping streets and docksides. A must (see pp64–7).

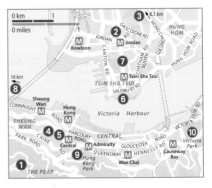

⑤ The Hong Kong Land Loop

MAP L5

Almost all of Central's prestige commercial towers are part of the portfolio of one company, Hong Kong Land, which has thoughtfully connected its properties with aerial walkways. The buildings include Jardine House, Mandarin Oriental, Princes Building and the Landmark Centre. Do the circuit, if only for the ethereal experience of experiencing downtown Hong Kong without ever touching the ground.

⑥ Cultural Centre Promenade

This walkway from the Kowloon Star Ferry, past the InterContinental, is notable for great views of Hong Kong Island's towers. See these lit to music nightly at 8pm in the Symphony of Lights show (see p88).

⑦ Nathan Road

A joyously tacky and tawdry strip, the Golden Mile, Hong Kong's own Broadway, runs up the Kowloon peninsula, passing hotels and tourist shops at the upscale southern end, before downgrading into the sleazy karaoke lounges and low-rent storefronts of central Kowloon. Just don't

Fishing boats at Cheung Chau

buy any of the cheap electronics along the way (see p85). If you need a respite from the hectic street life, stop off at Kowloon Park (see p87).

⑧ The Praya, Cheung Chau

This island praya (or waterfront road) is everything the main drag of a backwater fishing town should be: a rambling tableau of fresh catches, boats tying up, market stalls and skipping kids. Look out for the splendid hand-pulled water carts that are the island's only fire engines (see pp30–31).

⑨ The Central Green Trail

MAP L6

Just minutes from the towering banks, malls and offices of downtown, this signposted, hour-long trail from the Peak Tram terminus at Hong Kong Park opens up a lush hillside world of trees, ferns and rocks. A beautiful, shady walk that offers an alternative to taking the tram to the top.

⑩ Victoria Park

One of the city's larger green sites, Victoria Park is best visited in the early morning, when tai chi devotees exercise and it is at its most peaceful. Throughout the day there are people-watching opportunities and restful walks, away from the urban bustle (see p74).

Neon signs on Nathan Road

⟨TOP 10⟩ Areas of Natural Beauty

Sea birds at Mai Po Marsh nature reserve

① Cape D'Aguilar
MAP F6

It may be only 7 miles (11 km) directly south of Hong Kong's busy Central district, but Cape D'Aguilar feels like another world. The wild coastline has wave-lashed rock formations and a marine life so rich that researchers have discovered 20 new species in its waters.

② Hoi Ha Wan
MAP G2

The long inlets and sheltered coves of this marine park in northern Sai Kung are made for snorkelling. The water is full of stony coral and diverse species of colourful reef fish.

③ Mai Po Marsh

Declared a Ramsar site (that is, a wetland of international importance) in 1995, Mai Po is still one of China's most important bird sanctuaries, with hundreds of resident and migratory species recorded here, including many endangered ones. Other wildlife that live here include otters, civet cats, bats and amphibians (see p111). Tours organized by WWF on weekends.

④ Bride's Pool

The pool is a popular picnic spot. Weekends are best avoided, but visit midweek and, with luck, you will have this glorious, wooded course of rockpools and cascades all to yourself (see p111).

⑤ Pat Sin Range
MAP F2

Hong Kong's countryside achieves a quiet grandeur among the empty valleys and sublime uplands of Pat Sin ("eight spirits"). Peaks range up to 639 m (2,095 ft), and the views are humbling.

⑥ Jacob's Ladder
MAP G3

Take these steep steps up the rock from Three Fathom's Cove, and enter

an expanse of remote uplands and boulder-strewn paths, leading, in the north, to Mount Hallowes. There are exquisite views of the Tolo Channel.

7 Sha Lo Tung
MAP F2

This hidden valley in the New Territories is probably the closest Hong Kong comes to the stereo-typical idea of a classical Chinese landscape, with its old paddy fields, deserted villages, flowing streams and ancient woods. Magical.

White sand beaches of Tai Long Wan

Walkers on the Dragon's Back

8 Dragon's Back
MAP F5

This undulating ridge snakes down Hong Kong Island's south-east corner, with plunging slopes, poetic sea views and (past Pottinger's Gap) deep wooded valleys and beaches.

9 Tai Long Wan

On the Sai Kung Peninsula, survive the knuckle-whitening ascent of Sharp Peak (all loose rocks and narrow paths), and the land plunges down to your well-earned reward: the sparkling waves and white sand beaches of Hong Kong's finest bay, Tai Long Wan *(see pp28–9)*.

10 Ma On Shan

The plateaus and grassy slopes that surround the 702-m-(2,303-ft-) high Ma On Shan ("Saddle Mountain") allow for splendid panoramic views of the mountainous countryside, without the insidious intrusion of city skyline in the distance. The effect is truly majestic and worth the climb *(see p111)*.

The peak of Ma On Shan

Ways to Experience the Real China

① Spend a Night at the Opera

Cantonese opera might sound discordant to the untrained ear, but make no mistake, this is a fine and ancient art. It combines song, mime, dancing, martial arts and fantastic costumes and make-up, and can go on for 6 hours or more. Call the Tourist Board (see p149) for details of performances.

Opera singer

② Feast on Dim Sum

Dim sum is commonly translated as "touch the heart", and after a few plates of these delicious meat- or vegetable-filled dumplings, it is easy to see why. The small steamed snacks are delivered on trolleys in bamboo baskets (see p57).

③ Ride on a Junk

 Tours depart from Tsim Sha Tsui Pier 2 & Central Pier 9; Harbour Discovery tour noon–4pm Mon–Fri (hourly); Stanley Village tour noon Sat & Sun; evening cruises 6:30–10:45pm daily ■ Advance booking advisable ■ 2116 8821 ■ Adm ■ www.aqualuna. com.hk

We've all seen the iconic images of junks, blood-red batwing sails unfurled as the sun sets over Victoria Harbour. Hand built in the Hong Kong shipyard of an 80-year-old master craftsman, the *Aqua Luna* is one of the last remaining sailing junks.

④ Visit a Market

Hong Kong's wet markets can bring on instant culture shock for those tourists who are more used to the more orderly atmosphere of home supermarkets. Wander through the bustling street stalls, past often gruesome butchers and fishmongers, as hawkers yell and housewives bargain.

⑤ Go for a Traditional Tonic

MAP N6 ■ Cnr Luard and Hennessy rds, Wan Chai

For a taste of the real China, try a bowl of tonic tea from a streetside stall. These bitter brews are concocted from herbs according to traditional Chinese medicinal principles of whether they are "cooling" or "heating". The Lo Cha Di Yat Ka counter in Wan Chai labels all its offerings in English.

⑥ Try Foot Reflexology

1/F Lai Shing Bldg, 13–19 Sing Woo Rd (and three other branches) ■ 2893 0199

Vice-like hands seek out pressure points linked to vital organs. The procedure is painful, and you might be embarrassed about your feet, but you will feel so good when they stop. Reflexologists abound in Happy Valley. Try On Wo Tong.

⑦ Experience Unbelievable Gall

MAP K5 ■ Hillier St, Sheung Wan ■ 2543 8032

She Wong Lam in the northeast of Hong Kong Island is the best place to sup on snake wine, a traditional

Traditional junk, Victoria Harbour

winter tonic. The speciality is a fiery brew containing the gallbladders of five deadly snakes.

 Practise Tai Chi
MAP M4
Turn up at the Sculpture Court in front of the Museum of Art *(see p86)* in Tsim Sha Tsui at 8am on Mondays, Wednesdays and Fridays to enjoy an hour-long instruction in this gentlest of martial arts.

Chi Lin Nunnery, Kowloon

9 Aim for Everything Zen
For a modern take on ancient China, check out the Chi Lin Nunnery in Kowloon. This gorgeous replica of a seven-hall Tang dynasty (AD 618–907) complex took 10 years to build, using traditional techniques and materials. Bliss out listening to the nuns chanting to the Sakyamuni Buddha *(see p102)*.

10 Watch a Lion Dance
Lions are thought to ward off evil and bring luck, which explains why the opening of a new building

often features a fascinating display of youths dancing beneath a stylized lion's head. These performances are commonly seen around Chinese New Year *(see p60)*.

Lion dance

TOP 10 WAYS TO PAMPER YOURSELF

Chinese massage

1 Spa-ing Bout
2696 6682
Check into the Peninsula for a stress-busting retreat at the luxurious spa.

2 Rubbed the Right Way
On Wo Tong *(see Reflexology entry)*
Go for a deep-tissue Chinese massage and get the blood circulating.

3 Male Pampering
3717 2797
The Bliss Spa at W Hong Kong offers a range of treatments for men.

4 In a Lather
2825 4088
A Shanghai-style shave at the Mandarin Oriental will leave your face feeling like a baby's bottom.

5 Love Potion No. 9
Boost your staying power with a tonic drink from one of the many kerbside Chinese medicine shops.

6 Geomancing the Stone
Raymond Lo ▪ 2736 9568
Set your house and garden in tune with the elements with a private feng shui consultation.

7 Pins and Needles
On Wo Tong *(see Reflexology entry)*
Loosen up with an acupuncture session.

8 Detoxify
2143 6288
The 45-minute detox warming body wrap at the Spa L'Occitane is divine.

9 Put Your Feet Up
2825 4888
Fans rave about the traditional Shanghai pedicure from the spa at the Mandarin Oriental.

10 The Doctor Is In
Dr Troy Sing ▪ 2526 7908
Try some alternative medicine from a traditional Chinese doctor.

🔟 Off The Beaten Track

Mandarin's House in Largo do Lilau, Macau

1 Largo do Lilau, Macau
Mandarin's House: 10 Travessa de António da Silva ■ **Open 10am–6pm Mon, Tue & Thu–Sun** ■ **www.wh.mo/mandarinhouse/en**
This tiny cobbled square was one of the earliest districts settled by Portuguese, and there's a distinctly European flavour to the surrounding shuttered windows and stuccoed façades. Head to the beautifully restored 19th-century Mandarin's House nearby for a taste of Classical Chinese architecture.

2 Pineapple Dam
MAP E4
This is also known as Shing Mun Reservoir. There's an easy 2-hour walk here through the woodland around the water, with the chance to see macaques and birds. Bring lunch and make use of the barbecue sites, or extend your hike to Tai Mo Shan or Tai Po town.

3 Wing Wah Noodles
MAP N6 ■ **A89 Hennessy Road, Wan Chai** ■ **2527 7476**
Everyone in Hong Kong has a favourite wonton

noodle restaurant but this really is one of the best. A tiny, long-running affair whose crowd of chairs and tables makes for cosy dining. Their stock is excellent and the noodles are just right – soft but still resilient.

4 Hong Kong Cemetery
MAP F5 ■ **Wong Nai Chung Road, Causeway Bay** ■ **Open 8am–5pm daily**
Rising in terraces up the hillside opposite the racetrack, these cemeteries provide a snapshot of

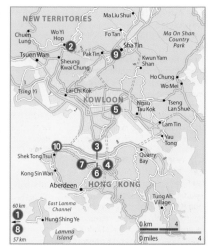

Hong Kong Cemetery

the people – Muslims, Christians, Parsees and Jews – who once settled this busy outpost. The Protestant section is the most atmospheric, overgrown with trees and crowded with Victorian-era mausoleums.

⑤ Sung Wong Toi
MAP E4 ■ Ma Tau Chung Road, Kowloon City

Though lacking in drama, Sung Wong Toi is a rare reminder that Hong Kong history far predates the British arrival in 1842. This boulder is the sole surviving fragment of a terrace once frequented by the last Song dynasty prince, who fled here to escape the 12th-century Mongol invasion of China.

⑥ Bowen Road
MAP E5

A short, exhausting walk uphill from busy Queens Road East in Wan Chai, Bowen Road is a narrow concrete strip that runs through unexpectedly thick forest, where traffic noise from below mingles with the humming of cicadas. Lovers' Rock, a phallic-shaped boulder poking rudely up through the treeline here, is a focus for the Maidens' Festival in August.

⑦ Nam Koo Terrace
MAP M6 ■ 55 Ship Street, Wan Chai

Reputedly the most haunted place in Hong Kong, this spooky, uninhabited, mouldering old Chinese mansion sits uncomfortably in the shadows of Wan Chai's towering skyscrapers, draped in strangler figs and the stalking grounds for an unlikely number of feral cats. Though a protected building, redevelopment plans are a real threat.

⑧ Three Lamps District

A bustling market area in the back lanes of northern Macau. Lanes radiating out from the Rotunda de Carlos da Maia are choked by stalls selling clothing, vegetables and all manner of daily necessities. On the periphery are some low-key temples and the Art Deco façade of the Red Market, where you can buy live meat for the cooking pot.

⑨ Tsang Tai Uk
MAP E4 ■ Near Lion Rock Tunnel Road, Sha Tin Wai

This small, old, Hakka clan mansion is strangely overlooked by visitors, despite being an easy walk from Sha Tin's Heritage Museum. Built by the Tsang family between the 1840s and the 1860s, the complex is well-preserved, with fortress-like walls and protective "tiger-fork" spikes on the roofs. Parts are still lived in today.

⑩ Lo Pan Temple
MAP E5 ■ 15 Ching Lin Terrace, Kennedy Town ■ 2802 2880

A short walk uphill from the Belcher's Bay Park tram stop, this small temple dates from 1884 and is the only one in Hong Kong dedicated to Lo Pan, the patron deity of carpenters. The two halls sport a gorgeous, ornate roof, decorated with figures made at the famous ceramics centre of Shiwan, in China.

Lo Pan Temple

🔟 Places for Children

Exhibit at the Science Museum

1 Science Museum

There is lots of hands-on stuff here, providing a fun and educational introduction to many facets of science. Any child with a healthy dose of curiosity will spend hours pushing buttons, pulling levers and marvelling at gadgets (see p86).

2 Ocean Park

"Connecting people with nature" is what it's all about at Ocean Park. The Giant Panda Habitat, Atoll Reef, Sea Jelly Spectacular and Dolphin University exhibits will keep children engrossed for hours. Older kids will love the supervised sessions where you can touch some of the animals. The park also features nearly 30 exciting rides, including The Dragon rollercoaster and Raging River water ride, plus a cable car (see p79).

3 Zoological and Botanical Gardens

MAP K6 ■ Albany Rd, Central ■ 6am–7pm daily ■ www.lcsd.gov.hk/en/parks/hkzbg

Founded in 1864, a modicum of Victorian gentility survives here in the wrought-iron bandstand and shrub-lined paths. Not, however, in the monkey house, where the world's largest collection of red-cheeked gibbons swing about the enclosure. Also look out for the orangutans, lemurs and 280 species of birds here.

Parade at Disneyland

4 Hong Kong Disneyland

Lantau Island, served by its own MTR station ■ 1-830-830 for hours and today's tickets ■ Adm ■ www.hongkongdisneyland.com for advance booking

Designers wisely used feng shui in the design of Disney's latest Asian venture, but otherwise there are few nods to local culture. Adventureland, Fantasyland and Tomorrowland lie beyond Main Street, USA.

The Dragon rollercoaster at Ocean Park

Ngong Ping 360 Cable Car

5 Ngong Ping 360 Cable Car

The spectacular 25-minute cable-car journey from the hustle and bustle of the city, across open water and up the steep hillside from Tung Chung to the Big Buddha at Po Lin (see pp32–3), is the best funfair ride in town (see p120).

6 Dolphin Watching

MAP B4 ▪ 2984 1414 ▪ Bus pick-up 8:50am at the Kowloon Hotel or boat pick-up 9:30am at Tung Chung New Development Pier, Lantau ▪ Wed, Fri, Sun ▪ Adm ▪ www.hkdolphinwatch.com

Be quick, because the sorry state of Hong Kong's waters is killing off the rare Indo-Pacific humpback dolphins, which here in the Pearl River delta are a pale-pink colour.

7 Lions Nature Education Centre

MAP G3 ▪ Tsiu Hang, Sai Kung, New Territories ▪ 2792 2234 ▪ 9:30am–5pm Wed–Mon

The Lions Nature Education Centre is more fun than it sounds, with fruit orchards, an arboretum, rock gardens and, best of all, an insectarium. Big brothers will find plenty of interesting creepy-crawlies with which to scare their little sisters.

8 Tram Tour

Rock, rattle and roll along the front of Hong Kong Island, or take a detour around Happy Valley. Hong Kong's trams may be crowded, slow and noisy, but they are terrific for sightseeing (see p141).

9 Kowloon Park

The green lungs of Tsim Sha Tsui have a huge indoor-outdoor swimming pool, lots of gardens and children's favourite, the Avenue of Comic Stars with life-size statues (see p87).

Avenue of Comic Stars, Kowloon Park

10 Hong Kong Wetland Park

MAP C2 ▪ Tin Shui Wai, New Territories ▪ 3152 2666 ▪ 10am–5pm Wed–Mon ▪ Adm ▪ www.wetlandpark.gov.hk

This landscaped wetlands area on the border with China has bird hides, a butterfly garden, lily ponds and a mangrove circuit featuring mud-skippers and fiddler crabs. There is also a great, informative walk-through environmental display.

🔟 Hong Kong for Free

Nan Lian Garden, Kowloon

① Parks and Gardens

Hong Kong's varied parks and gardens are all free. The pick of the sights include Hong Kong Park, with its excellent walk-through Edward Youde Aviary and the nearby Zoological and Botanical Gardens (see p48); the traditional Nan Lian Garden at Diamond Hill (see p102); and historic Kowloon Walled City Park, once the site of a lawless housing estate and now a peaceful garden (see p101).

Crested Pigeon, Edward Youde Aviary

② Harbour Views

Admire Hong Kong's busy harbour and dynamic architecture from a number of free viewpoints: The Peak offers the most impressive panoramas; the Bank of China building has free access to its 43rd-floor viewing platform (bring photographic ID); or watch the evening light show from the Tsim Sha Tsui waterfront.

③ Mid-Levels Escalator

For an effortless, free ride uphill through the busy market and entertainment district, catch the unique Mid-Levels Escalator

Martial artists in Kowloon Park

between Central and SoHo (see p65). You are rewarded with great views of historic architecture and vignettes of street life in the lanes below. Get off to shop for trinkets along the way on Hollywood Road.

④ Aberdeen Harbour Ferry

Hiring a junk for a half-hour ride around Aberdeen Harbour is a time-honoured way of glimpsing life on Hong Kong's largest fishing fleet, but bargain-hunters can enjoy a shorter version for free by catching a ferry out to one of the famous floating restaurants (see p79) – you don't need to be intending to dine.

⑤ Macau's Casinos

Macau's many casinos – there are 35 at the latest count – could prove to be a serious drain on your finances, but entry is free and they make splendid places to people-watch. Try the Grand Lisboa for ridiculous ostentation, the Sands Cotai for routine glitz, the Venetian for its scale and film-set canals, and the Kam Pek for hard-bitten Chinese punters (see p127).

⑥ Martial Arts

Martial arts are part of Hong Kong's culture but, despite what you'll see in the movies, the real thing tends to be hidden away from public view. You can strike lucky in the nearest park at dawn, or catch the free 2-hour shows held at Kowloon Park's Kung Fu Corner every Sunday afternoon (see p87).

7 Hiking

Hong Kong is covered in hiking trails; some of them are surprisingly tough and all wind through large swathes of the territory that have so far escaped development. Hong Kong Island's Dragon's Back trail offers an accessible, relatively easy introduction, and ends with a beach and supper at Shek O *(see p80)*.

8 Temples

Hong Kong's many temples are free to visit (although change for the collection box is appreciated). Try the Man Mo Temple on Hollywood Road *(see p67)*, the Tin Hau Temple off Nathan Road in Yau Ma Tei *(see p74)* or the Wong Tai Sin Temple in eastern Kowloon *(see p101)*.

Camping on Han Tin Wan beach

9 Camping

www.afcd.gov.hk/english/country/cou_vis/cou_vis.html
Surprisingly, for a city where even cramped, budget accommodation usually comes at a premium, there are 41 free campsites spread across Hong Kong's New Territories, and some of them are in spectacular settings. The downsides are that they operate on a first-come-first-served basis, are all fairly remote and have only basic facilities.

10 Cultural Events

For free performances go to the foyer of the Hong Kong Cultural Centre *(see p86)* on Thursday lunchtimes and some Saturdays. The Fringe Club *(see p70)* hosts free live music from local and visiting bands. There are also various free events in the area around the Hong Kong Observation Wheel in Central *(see p66)*.

TOP 10 MONEY-SAVING TIPS

Food stalls at a produce market

1 Food Stalls
For the cheapest meals, eat at the food stalls at the indoor produce markets.

2 Museum Wednesdays
Most of Hong Kong's museums offer free admission on Wednesdays.

3 Happy Valley Races
At only HK$10 for entry, Happy Valley Races offers an inexpensive night out.

4 Chungking Mansions
www.chungking-mansions.hk
The best deals on budget accommodation are offered by the basic hostels in Chungking Mansions.

5 Star Ferry
The cheapest way to cross Hong Kong harbour – and with spectacular views – is aboard the Star Ferry.

6 Octopus Card
www.octopus.com.hk/en
Save time and money on Hong Kong's public transport system with an Octopus Card.

7 Happy Hour
Many of Hong Kong's bars and clubs offer relatively inexpensive drinks during daily happy hours.

8 Hotel Shuttles
A free shuttle service runs from the Airport Express station in Kowloon to Tsim Sha Tsui's hotels.

9 Shenzen Airport
Shenzhen airport offers cheaper flights into China than those from Hong Kong.

10 Markets and Malls
For the best prices on electronics, clothes, antiques and souvenirs, check out dedicated markets and malls.

TOP10 Nightclubs

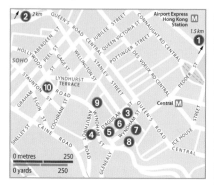

floor 118 of the Ritz-Carlton, with outdoor seating and impressive Victoria Harbour views.

3 Magnum
MAP K5 ▪ 3&4/F, 1 Wellington St, Central ▪ 2116 1602

Located in the heart of Central, Magnum Club is a two-storey monolith featuring transparent staircases, a bubble-like DJ booth and state-of-the-art sound system. There's a great bar (try the signature Magnum Club cocktail) with a glitter ball suspended above, an upstairs stage and, if the crowd gets too much, a rooftop terrace. Oh, and don't miss the gold-plated toilets.

4 Dragon-i
Stunning interior design in mixed Chinese and Japanese style but with lots of New York thrown in across two completely different rooms. The Red Room dining room becomes a VIP lounge for the famous as the evening progresses, with everyone else sinking into the booths in the bronze and mirrored "Playground", drinking powerful cocktails. This is a nightspot for the stylish set, so you'll need to dress accordingly (see p70).

1 Felix
The shining pinnacle of Hong Kong bars is set in Kowloon's famous Peninsula Hotel. Philippe Starck designed Felix, and the result is coolness incarnate. Let the experience envelop you, from the dedicated elevators and their light effects, to the untrammelled delights of the restrooms. The harbour views are an added bonus. If you plan to visit just one bar in Hong Kong, make this the one (see p91).

2 Ozone at the Ritz-Carlton
MAP L2 ▪ Ritz-Carlton Hong Kong, 1 Austin Rd W ▪ 2263 2263

Taking the honours as the highest bar in Hong Kong, Ozone sits on

Stylish interior at Ozone at the Ritz-Carlton

Plush bar area at Drop

(5) Volar

MAP K5 ■ Basement, 38–44 D'Aguilar St ■ 2810 1272

If you're in the mood to dance head to this intimate and loud basement venue that has become something of a nightlife institution since opening in 2004. Strips of LED neon lights run across the ceiling and walls and there is a state-of-the-art sound system. Enjoy a variety of dance music on Volar's two dance floors, including hip hop, house, electronica and more.

(6) Rúla Búla

The name of this hip place derives from an Irish saying meaning uproar and commotions. It has a trendy urban warehouse feel, with exposed steal beams and unpainted walls. Sip inventive cocktails and dance into the early hours to a mix of hip hop, pop and house music *(see p70)*.

(7) Play

MAP K5 ■ 1 On Hing Terrace, Central ■ 2525 1318

Hong Kong's largest single-floor nightclub lies in the heart of Central. It is split into three distinctive rooms, including two main rooms and a champagne bar. Top DJs and Asia's finest cocktail mixologists keep the trendy club clientele partying into the early hours of the morning.

(8) Fly

MAP K5 ■ 9/F 24–30 Ice House St, Central ■ 2810 9902

Playfully designed, this smart but unstuffy club with a contemporary interior is great for a night of non-stop electronic music. The thumping Turbosound system pumps out a mix of international DJ tunes, ranging from house and electric to dubstep and drum 'n' bass.

(9) Di Vino

MAP K5 ■ 73 Wyndham St, Central ■ 2167 8883

This tunnel-shaped wine bar and restaurant, crammed with beautiful people, makes the perfect start to any evening. There are special prices on early-evening aperitifs and around 40 wines available by the glass. The menu offers bar snacks and memorable Italian food designed for sharing.

(10) Drop

MAP K5 ■ 39–43 Hollywood Rd ■ 2543 8856

This super-hip venue is one of the best clubs in Hong Kong. Set up by resident DJ Joel Lai, it is the place to go to dance and see Hong Kong's "beautiful people". Though small in size, it has a large bar and is extremely popular, due in part to the special club events, happy hours and top DJs. It has a sister club in Shanghai.

🔟 Restaurants

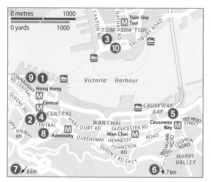

culinary traditions with distinctive Asian influences without ever becoming "fusion". This restaurant is simply outstanding, as its three Michelin stars imply, and is renowned especially for meat and seafood dishes *(see p71)*.

① Caprice

A three-star Michelin restaurant with views of the harbour, this is fine French dining at its most sumptuous; expect outstanding cuisine, excellent Bordeaux and Burgundy wines and lavish decor. Set-menu lunches draw a strong business crowd, while evenings and weekend lunches are definitely "see and be seen" affairs *(see p71)*.

Three-Michelin-starred Caprice

② L'Atelier de Joël Robuchon

L'Atelier is a highly contemporary venue decorated in bright scarlet with high-top seats arranged around an open kitchen. The set menu options combine classic French

③ T'ang Court

MAP N4 ▪ 2/F Langham Hotel, 8 Peking Road, Kowloon ▪ 2132 7898 ▪ $$$

The food at T'ang Court, the Langham Hotel's two-star Michelin restaurant, continues to astonish. Peerless creativity and insistence on *wok chi* (wok cooking at the highest achievable temperature) are the keys to its greatness.

④ 8½ Otto e Mezzo Bombana

This superb contemporary Italian restaurant was upgraded from two to three Michelin stars in 2011, the first Italian restaurant outside Italy to achieve that recognition. Chef Umberto Bombana, dubbed "The King of White Truffles", weaves his culinary magic using only the freshest ingredients. The name is taken from Italian director Federico Fellini's 1963 Oscar-winning autobiographical film *(see p71)*.

⑤ Kung Tak Lam

MAP P5 ▪ World Trade Center 1001, 208 Gloucester Rd, Causeway Bay ▪ 2890 3127 ▪ $

Vegetarians unable to face another helping of the slop and swill that passes for much meat-free cuisine in Hong Kong will praise the Creator for Kung Tak Lam. This light and airy Shanghainese does things with vegetables that could not be done, could not even be imagined, by most vegetarian restaurants elsewhere. Other branches are in Tsim Sha Tsui and Sha Tin.

The Verandah

6 The Verandah

From its epic Sunday brunches through to romantic, candle-lit dinners, this Southside patrician enjoys impeccable service and a well-deserved lead over nearby competition. The elegant interior has views through shuttered windows of tree-tops and the sea. Go for the fresh oysters and the Grand Marnier soufflé (see p83).

7 Top Deck

The Jumbo floating restaurant may be a tourist trap, but the top floor has been converted into a fantastic alfresco restaurant. Top Deck is a first-class seafood venue, serving everything from soft-shelled crab tempura to tasty bouillabaisse (see p83).

Duck liver and baby salad, Gaddi's

8 Island Tang

The 1920s period decor and Cantonese teahouse menu appear smart and simple, though ingredients such as bird's nest and abalone hint at high standards. Superior dim sum, good Peking duck and roast meats are served here, along with plenty of vegetarian options. Island Tang also boasts an impressive wine cellar with some good vintages (see p71).

9 Lung King Heen

The world's first Chinese to earn three Michelin stars is a beautifully styled modern Cantonese restaurant. Lung King Heen means "View of the Dragon" and the inside is designed to replicate a Chinese landscape. It is particularly strong on seafood dishes and dim sum, which can be enjoyed while taking in the splendid harbour views (see p71).

10 Gaddi's

Royalty, Hollywood stars and heads of state have all been known to dine here. In terms of French cuisine in the city, Gaddi's is the holy grail. Expect the highest level in every area: from the sophisticated menu to ultra-attentive service. If you are a fan of haute cuisine, you've found your heaven (see p91).

Opulent dining room at Gaddi's

For a key to restaurant price ranges see p71

🔟 Hong Kong Dishes

Plate of *cha siu*

1 Cha Siu
This is virtually Hong Kong's national dish. The name literally means "fork roast". The tender fillets of pork are roasted and glazed in honey and spices, and hung in the windows of specialist roast meat shops. *Cha siu* is classically served thinly sliced, with steamed rice and strips of vegetables.

Traditional moon cake

2 Moon Cake
Made of moist pastry and various fillings, including lotus, taro, adzuki bean, whole egg yolk and occasionally coconut, the delicacy also has a quirky history: revolutionaries in imperial China used to smuggle messages to each other hidden in the cake's dense filling.

3 Steamed Whole Fish
In Hong Kong, fish is almost always dressed very simply, using only peanut oil, soya sauce, chives and coriander. To maximize freshness, restaurants keep tanks of live fish, which are prepared to order.

4 Hainan Chicken
Comprising chunks of steamed chicken, served slightly warm or cold, dipped in an aromatic oil made with spring onions and ginger, this dish has become everyday comfort food. It is traditionally accompanied by a rich chicken broth, a few vegetables and rice steamed in chicken stock for flavour.

5 Brisket of Beef
Requiring up to 8 hours of slow cooking, preparation of this Hong Kong classic is an art. Households and restaurants guard their individual recipes, but all involve the classic five Chinese spices, rock sugar and tangerine peel. It's served in an earthenware pot as a main course, or as a topping for rice or noodles. Given the dish's richness, it is particularly enjoyed during the cooler winter months.

6 Wontons
Done properly, these marvellous prawn and pork Chinese ravioli are poached in a stock made from shrimp roe, aniseed and other spices, and served with fresh egg noodles and soup.

7 Water Spinach
The leafy, hollow-stemmed vegetable can be prepared with various seasonings, from the quotidian oyster sauce to garlic and shrimp paste. At its best when stir-fried with potent chillies and semi-fermented tofu.

Fried water spinach with chilli

8 Fish Balls

A daily food for many Hong Kongers, either on skewers as snacks or served with noodles in broth to make a meal. Traditional restaurants eschew machine production methods, and still shape these balls of minced fish, white pepper and other spices by hand, before poaching them in seafood or chicken stock.

Fish balls in curry sauce

9 Salt and Pepper Crusted Squid

You may have encountered the disastrous and greasy travesty of fried squid served up in Western Chinatowns. Banish that unpleasant memory from your mind, and prepare to discover the gloriously crisp original. Fresh squid is scored, lightly battered and flash fried with lots of salt, white pepper, chilli and garlic. The result is an addictive combination of tangy textures.

10 Lai Wong Bau

Chinese bread is shaped into buns, not loaves, and steamed rather than baked – giving it a beautifully soft and fluffy quality (no gritty whole grains here). There are many varieties of Chinese sweet bun, but *lai wong bau* is the reigning favourite, the kind of treat that children will clamour for. These buns are filled with a mixture of milk, eggs, coconut and sugar. Try them piping hot on a cold winter morning.

TOP 10 DIM SUM (DUMPLINGS)

Dim sum in steaming baskets

1 Har Gow
Prawns wrapped in a rice-flour casing and then steamed – like a very plump, transparent ravioli.

2 Siu Mai
Traditional minced pork and shrimp parcels, topped with a dab of crab roe or diced carrot.

3 Seen Juk Guen
Soy pastry, crisp fried with a vegetable filling. A savvy alternative to the common spring roll.

4 Gai Jaht
Chicken and ham wrapped in soya-bean sheets, served in rich sauce.

5 Lohr Bahk Goh
Shredded Chinese radish, pan-fried with chives, dried shrimp and Chinese salami, then steamed to form a "cake".

6 Cheung Fun
Rolls of rice pastry, filled with shrimp, pork or beef, and smothered in sweet soy sauce.

7 Chiu Chow Fun Gohr
Soft, pasty-style dumplings filled with chopped nuts, minced pork and pickled vegetables.

8 Chin Yeung Laht Jiu
Green pepper stuffed with minced fish and prawns and served in black-bean sauce.

9 Ji Ma Wu
Decadent, treacle-like dessert made from sugar and mashed sesame. It is served warm from the trolley.

10 Ma Lai Goh
Wonderfully light and fluffy steamed sponge cake, made with eggs, brown sugar and walnuts.

TOP10 Markets

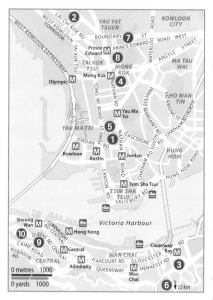

possibly an impromptu Chinese Opera recital (see pp22–3).

2 Apliu Street Flea Market

This flea market at Sham Shui Po is a treasurehouse of secondhand household goods and utter junk, strewn either side of the pavement in makeshift stalls. It's the most fun of Hong Kong's street markets, not least because you just might uncover one of the genuine vintage collectables that occasionally surfaces here. It's also a place to pick up pre-loved mobile phones and electronic gadgetry (see p102).

1 Temple Street

This atmospheric market comes alive at night. Hundreds of stalls are jam-packed by 9pm, offering pirated goods and all manner of, well, junk. It used to be known as Men's Street, and many stalls still stock less-than-fashionable attire. Venture past the market and you'll stumble onto a lamplit coterie of fortune tellers and

3 Jardine's Bazaar and Jardine's Crescent

MAP Q6 ▪ Jardine's Bazaar, Causeway Bay, Hong Kong Island ▪ 11am–8pm

An open-air market area in the heart of Causeway Bay, one of Hong Kong's busiest shopping districts. All sorts of goodies here, from run-of-the-mill fashion shops to traditional barbers and Chinese medicine sellers. Try a glass of fresh soy bean milk.

Market trader selling masks at Temple Street Market

Shoppers at Ladies' Market

Kong's odder fashion statements). A colourful flower market is just down the road *(see p93)*.

8 Goldfish Market
MAP E4 ■ Tung Choi St, Mong Kok ■ 10am–6pm

A popular spot for locals, as a fishtank in the right spot is thought to ward off bad luck. Hook a bargain on underwater furniture with an Oriental flavour, or just admire the colourful creatures on show.

9 Gage Street
MAP K5

It's a shock to find Gage Street's crush of down-to-earth market stalls just a stone's throw from Central's sophisticated boutiques. You might want to avoid the confrontational butcher's shops, but it's worth a visit to see how ordinary Hong Kongers buy their groceries.

4 Ladies' Market
No designer labels – unless they're fake. What you'll find here is inexpensive women's clothing from lingerie to shoes. There's a decent selection of jeans, plus cheap food and knick-knacks galore *(see p95)*.

5 Jade Market
As you might suppose, jade sellers abound – more than 450 of them at the last count. Don't attempt to buy the top-grade stuff unless you're an expert and know what you are doing. But there are plenty of cheaper pieces to be found *(see p94)*.

Pendant, Jade Market

10 Cat Street
MAP J5

The name refers to the Chinese slang for "odds and ends". The market here and on nearby Hollywood Road are chock-full of antique and curio shops. This is the place to come for silk carpets, elegant Chinese furniture, Ming dynasty ceramic horsemen and Maoist kitsch.

6 Stanley Market
MAP F6 ■ Stanley Main St, Hong Kong Island ■ 10am–6pm

Full of tourists of the badge-sporting, flag-following variety, this can still be a fun place to shop. If you're not claustrophobic, join the hordes thronging the narrow lanes to gorge on tacky rubbish *(see p20)*.

7 Bird Garden
MAP N2 ■ Yuen Po Street, Mong Kok ■ 7am–8pm

More than 70 stalls showcasing and selling all manner of songbirds and (mostly legal) exotic species, bounded by elegant courtyards full of old men with white singlets rolled up to bare their bellies (one of Hong

Traditional dolls on Cat Street

🔟 Festivals and Events

Chinese dragon at Tin Hau Festival

① Tin Hau Festival
The 23rd day of the 3rd moon (Apr or May)

This is the big one if you make your living from the sea. Fishermen make floral paper offerings to Tin Hau, the goddess of the sea, hoping for fine weather and full nets. (Her views on overfishing and drag-netting aren't clear.) The best celebrations are at the temples at Stanley, Joss House Bay or Tin Hau Temple Road.

② Chinese New Year
Three days from the first day of the first moon, usually late Jan or early Feb

Hong Kong's most celebrated festival is a riot of neon and noise. Skyscrapers on both sides of the harbour are lit up to varying degrees, depending on the vicissitudes of the economy; fireworks explode over the harbour, shops shut down and doormen suddenly turn nice, hoping for a handout of *lai see* (lucky money).

③ Spring Lantern Festival (Yuen Siu)
The 15th day of the lunar calendar (end Feb)

Also known as Hong Kong's Valentine's Day, this festival marks the end of the traditional Chinese New Year celebrations. Beautiful glowing lanterns are hung in parks and flower markets, and couples stroll hand in hand.

④ Cheung Chau Bun Festival
MAP C6 ▪ The 6th day of the 4th moon (April or May), Cheung Chau

For four days, the island disappears under clouds of incense smoke and exuberant crowds. Highlights include a parade of children in period costumes, and a thrilling midnight race to scale 8-m- (26-ft-) high towers made of buns.

⑤ Mid-Autumn Festival
The 15th night of the 8th moon (Aug); try Victoria Park

Commemorating a 14th-century uprising against the Mongols, this family festival features colourful lantern displays in parks, the mass consumption of yolk-centred moon cakes and an extraordinary Fire-dragon Dance in Tai Hang district, where a 67-m-long dragon is run through the lanes at night.

Mid-Autumn Festival

⑥ Ching Ming
First week of Apr

Also known as the grave-sweeping festival, *ching ming* means "clear and bright". This is when Chinese families visit the graves of their ancestors to clear them of any weeds and wilted flowers. Many people also light incense and burn paper money.

⑦ Hungry Ghost Festival (Yue Laan)
Jul, various locations
From the 14th day of the seventh moon, the Chinese believe the gates of hell are thrown open and the undead run riot on earth for a month. Lots more "hell money" goes up in smoke, as do various hillsides. This is not a good time for hiking.

⑧ Dragon Boat Festival (Tuen Ng)
The 5th day of the 5th moon (early June); various venues
Drums thunder and paddles churn the waters of Hong Kong as garish craft vie for the top prize. The festival honours Qu Yuan, a 3rd-century poet-statesman who drowned himself to protest against corrupt rulers.

Competitors, Dragon Boat Festival

⑨ Art Basel Hong Kong
Held annually, dates vary
■ www.artbasel.com
This significant festival in the contemporary art world sees galleries from all over Asia and the Asia-Pacific come together. Highly regarded, it gives new and established artists a pivotal platform from which to showcase their work.

⑩ Christmas Day
25th Dec
Not a traditional Chinese festival, of course, but Hong Kongers have wholeheartedly embraced the more commercial aspects of Christmas.

TOP 10 SPORTING EVENTS

Macau Grand Prix

1 Lunar New Year Cup
Hong Kong Stadium ■ www.hkfa.com ■ Feb
A Hong Kong football team goes head to head against international competition.

2 Rugby Sevens
www.hksevens.com ■ Mar/Apr
Fast rugby and beer-fuelled mayhem.

3 Cricket Sixes
Kowloon Cricket Club ■ www.hkcricket.org ■ Oct
Top players take part in action around the stumps. Check website as the event has been cancelled in the past.

4 International Dragon Boat Races
Sha Tin ■ Mid-Jun
Festive boats compete on the Shing Mun River.

5 International Races
Sha Tin Racecourse ■ 2966 8335 ■ www.sha-tin.com ■ Dec
Spectacular, high-profile equine competition.

6 HK Badminton Open
Hong Kong Coliseum ■ 2504 8318 ■ Nov
International badminton stars.

7 Standard Chartered Hong Kong Marathon
2577 0800 ■ www.hkmarathon.com ■ Jan/Feb
The gruelling race covers the entire city.

8 Macau Grand Prix
www.macau.grandprix.gov.mo ■ Nov
Formula 3 action in the former Portuguese enclave.

9 Oxfam Trailwalker
2520 2525 ■ Nov
A gruelling walk over MacLehose Trail.

10 Hong Kong Open
Asian PGA 2621 6000 ■ Nov
Prestigious annual golf tournament.

Hong Kong
Area by Area

View of Central's skyline
from Victoria Peak

🔟 Hong Kong Island – Northwest

Water Buffalo by Elisabeth Frink, Exchange Square

From the corporate vanities of Central district's glass towers, through the vodka bars and galleries of SoHo, and spilling down flagstone lanes to the raucous shophouses and old docksides of Western, the Island's northwest potently concentrates all of Hong Kong's surreal contradictions. In the concrete gullies between futuristic banks and statement office blocks you'll find traditional street markets, temples and herbalists, all carrying on like some Hollywood dream of old Chinatown. These are some of the most mercantile streets in human history. A shot of snake-bile wine, or a fierce macchiato? In this part of the city, you can have it all.

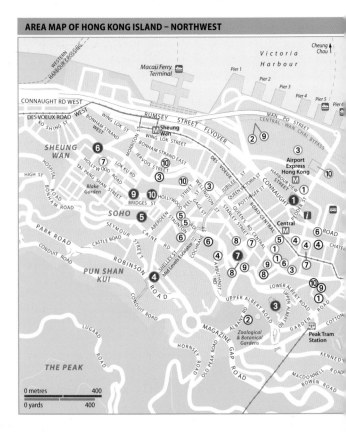

AREA MAP OF HONG KONG ISLAND – NORTHWEST

1 Exchange Square
MAP L5

As the name suggests, Exchange Square houses Hong Kong's red-carpeted financial engine room, although the stock exchange is not open to visitors. However, the peaceful square outside it, dominated by a large fountain, is a great place to picnic. Near the fountain are sculptures by Henry Moore and Dame Elisabeth Frink. The square's tallest building, Two IFC Tower (see pp38–9), was designed by Cesar Pelli.

2 Hong Kong Park
MAP L6

This park's open spaces and mature trees make an excellent escape, particularly the strikingly elegant

Hong Kong Park and aviary

(and free) walk-through aviary. The flowing streams and lush plant life of this improbable mini-rainforest are a peaceful and shaded home to scores of exotic bird species. The park also has lakes, a large conservatory, a viewing tower and the free Museum of Teaware, inside Flagstaff House.

3 Former Government House
MAP L6

This grand old building served as the British governor's residence from 1855 until 1997, when the last governor, Chris Patten, handed Hong Kong back to China. Patten's successor, Tung Chee-hwa, cited bad feng shui created by the needle-like Bank of China Tower (see p38) as one reason not to move in, opting to remain in his house on the Peak. Back in the 1940s, the occupying Japanese added the Shinto-style towers to the Georgian structure, which at one time enjoyed harbour views. It is used for official functions, only open occasionally to the public – contact HKTB (see p145) for details.

4 The Escalator
MAP K5

A wonderful feature of Hong Kong is its 792-m- (2,598-ft-) long string of escalators, which links all the roads between Queen's Road and Conduit Street. It's the best way for pedestrians to get around the steep districts of Central, the Mid-Levels and SoHo. The Escalator runs uphill until midnight, except during the morning rush hour, when it runs downhill.

Peng Chau, Mui Wo

Star Ferry Pier

1 Top 10 Sights
see pp65–7

1 Restaurants
see p71

1 Up-Market Malls and Boutiques
see p69

1 Bars and Clubs
see p70

1 Colonial Relics
see p68

(under construction)

8

WATERFRONT

LUNG WUI ROAD

EDINBURGH PLACE

CENTRAL RD

CHUNG WAN (CENTRAL)

Tamar Park

Chater Garden

Admiralty **M**

GLOUCESTER ROAD

ARSENAL ST

TAMAR ST

DRAKE ST

7
8

QUEENSWAY

SUPREME COURT RD

HENNESSY RD

QUEEN'S RD EAST

STAR STREET

TREE DRIVE

ROAD

2
2
2

KENNEDY ROAD

5

BOWEN ROAD

SoHo
MAP J–K5

Since the late 1990s SoHo (so-called for being the area south of Hollywood Road) has been transformed from a sleepy district of traditional Chinese shops into a thriving area for hip bars, cafés and restaurants. Elgin, Shelley and Staunton streets are excellent places to find a drink or bite to eat at any time of day.

6 Sheung Wan and Western
MAP J4

The older, more traditional Chinese areas of town, just west of Central's sleek corporate headquarters and the smart shops, are worth exploring by foot. The reward is a fascinating array of shops, mostly wholesalers, selling dried seafood (the pervading smell here), ginseng, edible swallows' nests, snakes, arcane herbal ingredients and paper offerings for the dead. Try the streets around Bonham Strand.

7 Lan Kwai Fong
MAP K5

Not much to look at during the day, Lan Kwai Fong (or Orchid Square) only really starts to buzz at night when office workers, including plenty of city suits, come here to unwind at its many restaurants,

PLAGUE

In the 19th century, Hong Kong, like many other parts of the world in history, suffered devastating plagues incubated in filthy, crowded slums. It was also in Hong Kong where, in 1894, the source of the plague was identified, almost simultaneously, by two doctors. The discovery of the bacteria went on to revolutionize prevention and treatment of plague.

bars and clubs. The street is packed with revellers on Fridays. The partying spills across to tiny Wing Wah Lane, just across D'Aguilar Street, with bars and a decent selection of good-value Thai, Malay and Indian restaurants.

8 The Waterfront
MAP L–M5 ■ Hong Kong Observation Wheel: Open 10am–11pm daily; Adm; www.hkow.hk

Turn right out of the Central Star Ferry for some open waterside space and benches with good views across to Kowloon. To the east is the 60-m (197-ft) high Hong Kong Observation Wheel, a Ferris wheel that offers great views of the harbour. The waterfront hosts A Symphony of Lights, the laser-and-sound show that lights up the buildings around the harbour every evening at 8pm.

The Waterfront, seen from across the harbour in Kowloon

Man Mo Temple

⑨ Man Mo Temple
MAP J5 ■ Western end,
Hollywood Rd

The gloomy red-and-gold interior of the Man Mo Temple, dating back to the 1840s, is always thick with sandalwood smoke from the giant incense spirals hanging overhead, which take a couple of weeks to burn through. The temple is dedicated to two deities, Man (the god of literature) and Mo (the god of war). Some of the scenes from the 1960 film version of Richard Mason's *The World of Suzie Wong* were filmed here.

⑩ Hollywood Road
MAP J–K5

This mecca for Chinese antiques and curios may no longer offer the bargains it once did, but Hollywood Road's eastern end is still jammed with shops selling ancient ceramics, mammoth ivory carvings and delicate snuff bottles. The stalls and shops on Upper Lascar Row are a good hunting ground for old coins, antiques, trinkets, kitsch and curios. Some art galleries have also opened here.

**Buddha figure,
Hollywood Road**

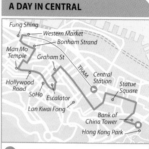

A DAY IN CENTRAL

Fung Shing
Western Market
Bonham Strand
Man Mo
Temple   Graham St
TRAM   Central
Station   Statue
Hollywood   Square
Road
SoHo   Escalator
Lan Kwai Fong
Bank of
China Tower
Hong Kong Park

▶ MORNING

From Des Voeux Road take the tram westwards from Central and jump off outside the handsome colonial building housing **Western Market**. Browse among the ground-floor trinkets or select a pattern from the many bolts of material on the first floor. The nearby Fung Shing restaurant serves excellent dim sum.

The streets around nearby **Bonham Strand** contain dried-seafood shops, Chinese apothecaries, and paper offering shops. Head uphill to the atmospheric **Man Mo Temple**, then east past the antique shops of **Hollywood Road**, browsing the stalls as you go.

Break for lunch or a drink in one of the many restaurants and bars on the streets to the south of (**SoHo**) or below Hollywood Road in **Lan Kwai Fong**.

AFTERNOON

Check out the fresh produce market stalls around the **Escalator** *(see p65)* and Graham Street before hitting **Statue Square** *(see pp14–15)*, the Island's colonial heart.

Choose to visit the **up-market malls** *(see p69)*, or for some peace and harbour views head to Queen's Pier, or for altitude and a spectacular city perspective go up to the viewing gallery high in the imposing, needle-sleek **Bank of China Tower** *(see p38)*.

Quiet and shade are found in the nearby **Hong Kong Park** *(see p65)*.

See map on pp64–5

Colonial Relics

Nave of St John's Cathedral

1 St John's Cathedral
MAP L6 ■ 4–8 Garden Road

Resembling a parish church more than a cathedral, St John's, completed in 1850, is the oldest Anglican church in east Asia.

2 George VI Statue
MAP K6

This statue, erected in 1941 in Hong Kong's Zoological and Botanical Gardens *(see p48)*, commemorated 100 years of British rule.

3 Colonial Street Names
MAP K5–6

Most colonial buildings have been sacrificed to new development, but the colonial legacy is preserved in many of the roads named after royals (Queen's Road), politicians (Peel Street), military officers (D'Aguilar, Pedder) and public servants (Bonham, Des Voeux).

4 Old Letter Box
MAP L5

A few traditional green, cast-iron post boxes bearing the British royal cipher remain. There is one at the northern end of Statue Square.

5 Former Military Hospital
MAP L6 ■ Bowen Road

Broken into separate units – some abandoned – the huge, grand old

The handsome Former French Mission

building, built from 1903 to 1906 between Bowen and Borrett roads, used to serve as a military hospital.

6 Hollywood Road Police Station
MAP K5

Bastions of colonial law and order, the Police Station (1864) and the old Victoria Prison (1841) still stand.

7 Flagstaff House
MAP L6 ■ Hong Kong Park

Built in the mid-1840s, Flagstaff House is one of the oldest colonial buildings on the island and houses the free Museum of Teaware.

8 Duddell Street
MAP K5 ■ Off Ice House St

While not spectacular, the gas lamps and old steps of Duddell Street date back to the 1920s.

9 Court of Final Appeal
MAP L5

The elegant 1911 Neo-Classical building served as Hong Kong's Supreme Court and then as its Legislative HQ until the Court of Final Appeal relocated here in 2015.

George VI statue

10 Former French Mission
MAP L6 ■ Battery Path

This red-brick building was built in 1843 as the home of the first governor of Hong Kong. Restyled as the French Mission HQ in 1917, it later housed the Court of Final Appeal.

Up-Market Malls and Boutiques

Luxury boutiques at The Landmark Centre

 The Landmark Centre
MAP L5 ▪ Pedder St
A modern mall with conspicuous consumables from the likes of Chanel, Dior, Zegna, Paul Smith, Prada, Vuitton, Bulgari and Tiffany.

2 Harvey Nichols
MAP M6 ▪ Pacific Place, 88 Queensway, Admiralty
Designer clothes, cosmetics, gifts and food at the Hong Kong branch of the luxury British department store.

3 Lane Crawford
MAP L4 ▪ IFC Mall, 8 Finance St
Upmarket clothing, with concessions from most big Western designer brands, house-ware, beauty products, glass and porcelain, and Asia's largest women's shoe shop.

 The Prince's Building
MAP L5 ▪ Statue Square & Des Voeux Rd
Not as many top names as The Landmark Centre next door, but the bright, airy and less crowded Prince's Building is worth a visit if big-name clothes and accessory designers are your thing.

5 G.O.D.
MAP K5 ▪ 48 Hollywood Rd, Central
Goods of Desire is an ultra-hip store that offers an off-beat selection of Chinese-inspired furnishings, accessories and clothing.

6 Gucci
MAP L5 ▪ The Landmark Centre, G1
This beautiful temple to the brand of Gucci is tended by elegant priestesses. It's merely a question of whether you can afford to worship here.

7 Dragon Culture
MAP K5 ▪ 231 Hollywood Rd
Antiques shop with pottery from most dynasties, bamboo carvings and snuff bottles.

8 Lock Cha Tea Shop
MAP L6 ▪ G/F K.S.Lo Gallery, Hong Kong Park, Admiralty
All the tea in China (well, 100 varieties anyway), along with traditional and modern teaware, all sold by experts in a colonial-era building. Also, try the tasty dim sums.

9 Shanghai Tang
MAP K–L5 ▪ 1 Duddell St, Central
Local entrepreneur David Tang is behind this international brand, which takes a smart twist on traditional Chinese clothes and ornaments. Jackets and kitsch Mao watches are staples.

 Two IFC
MAP L5 ▪ 8 Finance St, Central
Hong Kong's smartest mall features a selection of top brands, including an Apple Store. There is also a superb supermarket and a cinema.

See map on pp64–5

Bars and Clubs

The smart interior of MO Bar at the Mandarin Oriental

1 **MO Bar**
MAP L5 ■ The Landmark
Mandarin Oriental, 15 Queen's Rd,
Central ■ 2132 0077
The glamorous bar at the legendary
Mandarin Oriental is the place to go
for cocktails, and all-day dining. It is
also a sophisticated night spot.

2 **Café Gray Deluxe**
MAP M6 ■ 49/F The Upper
House Hotel, Pacific Place, 88
Queensway ■ 3868 1106
This swanky cocktail and wine
lounge at the swish Upper House
Hotel has superb harbour views.

3 **Sense 99**
MAP K5 ■ 2/F, 99 Wellington St,
Central ■ 9466 4695
Hong Kong's favourite hangout
with live music. Rub shoulders with
musicians and artists in this pre-war
venue off the main strip.

4 **Dragon-i**
MAP K5 ■ UG/F The Centrium,
60 Wyndham St ■ 3110 1222
The most happening club in Central,
where models, movers and shakers
and celebrities from Jackie Chan to
Sting have been spotted.

5 **The Globe**
MAP K5 ■ 45–53A Graham St,
Central ■ 2543 1941
Hong Kong's best beer bar serves
locally micro-brewed beers and rare
tap beers from around the world.

6 **Feather Boa**
MAP K5 ■ 38 Staunton St, SoHo
■ 2857 2586
A former antiques shop, now a bar,
but with much of its old stock left in
situ. Like drinking in a camp
relative's front room.

7 **Sevva**
MAP L5 ■ 25/F Prince's
Building, 10 Chater Rd, Central
■ 2537 1388
Bonnie Gokson's beautifully designed
bar and restaurant is among the
city's most stylish hangouts.

8 **Rúla Búla**
MAP K5 ■ G/F, 58–62 D'Aguilar
Street, Lan Kwai Fong, Central
■ 2179 5225
This hip club is popular with expats
and features great DJs, a large dance
floor and excellent signature cocktails.

9 **Fringe Club**
MAP K6 ■ 2 Lower Albert Rd,
Central ■ 2521 7251
Hong Kong's alternative arts venue
offers a respite from Lan Kwai
Fong's rowdier beer halls. It hosts
live music, theatre and exhibitions.

10 **Zoo Bar**
MAP K5 ■ 33 Jervois St, Sheung
Wan ■ 3583 1200
Pioneering the trendification of this
area, the Zoo Bar is a natural pit stop
for anyone after a good time. Though
it is a gay bar, everyone is welcome.

Restaurants

1 Lei Garden

MAP K5 ■ Shop 3008, 3/F IFC Mall ■ 2295 0238 ■ $$

This multi-award-winning chain-restaurant serves modern Cantonese food as it should be – light, delicate and subtle.

2 Lung King Heen

MAP L4 ■ Four Seasons Hotel, 8 Finance St, Central ■ 3196 8880 ■ $$$

Executive chef Chan Yan Tak is the mastermind behind this contemporary Cantonese restaurant, which has earned three Michelin stars *(see p55)*.

Lung King Heen dining room

3 Island Tang

MAP L6 ■ Shop 222, The Galleria, 9 Queen's Rd, Central ■ 2526 8798 ■ $$$

Cantonese dishes and Chinese *haute cuisine* at Sir David Tang's restaurant *(see p55)*.

4 8½ Otto e Mezzo Bombana

MAP L5 ■ 202 Landmark Alexandria, 5–17 Des Voeux Rd, Central ■ 2537 8859 ■ $$$

Three Michelin stars says it all, for this is Italian gastronomy of the highest quality *(see p54)*.

5 L'Atelier de Joël Robuchon

MAP L5 ■ 315 & 401 The Landmark, Central ■ 2166 9000 ■ $$$

Superstar chef Joël Robuchon picks up Michelin stars almost wherever he sets up a restaurant. Expect perfectly executed French classics with a hint of Asian flair *(see pp54)*.

PRICE CATEGORIES

For a three-course meal for one with half a bottle of wine and extra charges. Prices are quoted in Hong Kong dollars.

$ under $250 **$$** $250–600 **$$$** over $600

6 The Mandarin Grill & Bar

MAP L5 ■ Mandarin Oriental, 5 Connaught Rd ■ 2825 4004 ■ $$$

The interior may have been revamped by Sir Terence Conran, but the menu still features English classics and premium seafood. It's held its Michelin star since 2009.

7 Jimmy's Kitchen

MAP K5 ■ 1–3 Wyndham St ■ 2526 5293 ■ $$

A favourite for its naff decor and retro menu, Jimmy's has been dishing out comfort food since 1928.

8 Yung Kee

MAP K5 ■ 32–40 Wellington St ■ 2522 1624 ■ $$

From its headset-toting waitresses to its efficient poultry kitchen (try the roast goose), Yung Kee is a riotous operation.

9 Caprice

MAP L4 ■ 6/F Four Seasons Hotel, 8 Finance St ■ 3196 8860 ■ $$$

Head chef Vincent Thierry and his team prepare modern French food in an open kitchen at this superb restaurant *(see p54)*.

10 Kau Kee

MAP J5 ■ 21 Gough St ■ 2815 0123 ■ No credit cards ■ Closed Sun ■ $

Humble Kau Kee was once offered millions of dollars for its beef brisket noodle recipe. Taste it and see why. This is a place of pilgrimage for foodies around the city and beyond.

See map on pp64–5

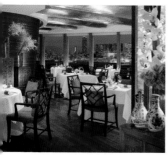

TOP 10 Hong Kong Island – Northeast

The famous Noonday Gun

The east of the island was the first to take up the population pressures of the nascent colonial capital of Victoria, and until the late 1970s had a low-rent reputation. Some of that survives in the haggard pole-dancing clubs and tattoo parlours of Wan Chai, where Richard Mason wrote *The World of Suzie Wong* and generations of sailors have nursed hangovers. But today, you're more likely to run into Starbucks. You'll see Hong Kongers at their most fevered at the Happy Valley night races, while in Causeway Bay is the neon of restaurants and boutiques. There are surprises among the warehouses and offices of Quarry Bay and Wan Chai – live jazz, microbreweries and dance clubs.

AREA MAP OF HONG KONG ISLAND – NORTHEAST

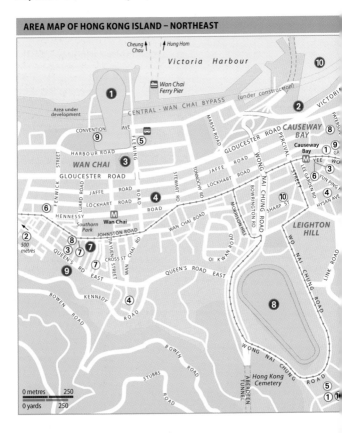

1 Convention and Exhibition Centre

MAP N5 ■ 1 Expo Drive, Wan Chai
■ 2582 8888 ■ www.hkcec.com

This building looks a bit like the Sydney Opera House might if its roof had just been swatted by a giant hammer. The vision of its designers was that the flowing lines would evoke a bird in flight. It is certainly a study in contrast, with the upthrust towers scratching the sky all around it. There was a race against time to finish stage two of the $5 billion complex in time for the 1997 Handover ceremony. Britain's loss and China's gain is commemorated with a big black obelisk. The venue also hosts occasional raves and pop concerts.

Convention and Exhibition Centre

2 Noonday Gun

MAP Q5 ■ Waterfront near the Causeway Bay typhoon shelter
■ To fire gun (for a fee): 2599 6111

Immortalized in Noël Coward's famous song about "Mad Dogs and Englishmen", the famous cannon has been fired at midday every day since 1860. Bigwigs pay for the privilege of firing it, with the money going to charity. Otherwise, a gunner dressed in traditional military attire does the honours.

3 Central Plaza

MAP N5 ■ 18 Harbour Rd, Wan Chai

Perhaps the developers figured "Central Plaza" had more cachet than "Wan Chai Plaza", or perhaps Wan Chai *is* central if you're talking about the mid-point of the waterfront. Anyway, Central Plaza is Hong Kong's third-tallest building (after Two IFC Tower and ICC Tower), standing at 374 m (1,227 ft).

4 Lockhart Road

MAP M–P6

Made famous in Richard Mason's novel *The World of Suzie Wong*, Wan Chai's sinful strip is these days an odd blend of girlie bars with doddery *mama-san* who saw action during the Vietnam War, down-at-heel discos, mock-British pubs and super-trendy bars and restaurants. The road is almost always being dug up, which adds to the hubbub.

The colourful interior of Tin Hau Temple

5 Tin Hau Temple
MAP R6 ■ 10 Tin Hau
Temple Rd, Causeway Bay
■ Open 7am–5pm daily

Not the biggest or best-known temple to the Chinese sea goddess, but certainly the most accessible. This was once the waterfront, believe it or not. There is usually a handful of worshippers burning incense and paying respects, although it may be packed during Chinese festivals.

6 Victoria Park
MAP Q–R5

Hong Kong's largest urban park opened in 1957 and features a statue of the British monarch, which an "art activist" once redecorated with red paint. There are tennis courts, lawn

Skyscrapers around Victoria Park

WHAT BECAME OF SUZIE WONG?

Many first-time visitors to Hong Kong have one image of Wan Chai fixed firmly in their heads – that of the Luk Kwok Hotel with its tarts-with-hearts and rickshaw-cluttered surrounds from the film of Richard Mason's novel *The World of Suzie Wong*. It's an image that's at least 40 years out of date. The original hotel was knocked down in 1988, and the soaring glass-and-steel tower that replaced it, bearing the same name, is full of offices and restaurants. Suzie might still survive, but if she does, she has gimlet eyes and a harridan's scowl.

bowling greens and a swimming pool. It's also the venue for the Chinese New Year Flower Market, and every Sunday at noon would-be politicians can stand up and shoot their mouths off at the forum.

7 "Old" Wan Chai
MAP N6

This could almost be labelled Hong Kong's "Little Thailand". Dozens of Thai mini-marts and hole-in-the-wall Thai restaurants have sprung up amid Wan Chai market in the narrow warren of lanes that run between Johnston Road and Queen's Road East. You can find the same dishes here for a quarter of what you'll pay in Thai restaurants just blocks away.

(8) Happy Valley Races

From September to June the thud of hooves on turf rings out most Wednesday nights from this famous racetrack – once a malaria-ridden swamp – where Hong Kong's gambling-mad public wager more money per meeting than at any other track in the world (see pp16–17).

(9) Hopewell Centre

MAP N6 ■ 183 Queen's Rd East, Wan Chai ■ 2574 6262 ■ The Grand Buffet: 2506 0888 ■ www.hopewellcentre.com

Construction mogul Gordon Wu has built roads in China and half-built a railway in Bangkok, but this remains his best-known edifice. The 64-storey cylinder makes diners dizzy in its revolving restaurant, The Grand Buffet, which, aside from the view, features one of the best buffet spreads in town. Night-times are most spectacular so be sure to book well in advance.

(10) Causeway Bay Typhoon Shelter

MAP Q5

Down-at-heel gin palaces and barnacle-encrusted hulks rub gunwales with multimillion-dollar yachts in this packed haven from the "big winds" that regularly bear down on the South China coast. There are also quaint houseboats with homely touches like flower boxes perman-ently anchored behind the stone breakwater. The impressive edifice to the left as you look out to sea is the Royal Hong Kong Yacht Club.

Causeway Bay Typhoon Shelter

A DAY IN NORTHEAST HONG KONG ISLAND

[map: Convention and Exhibition Centre, Excelsior Hotel, Victoria Park, Pacific Place, Lockhart Road, TRAM / MTR, Causeway Bay Station, Hennessy Road, Times Square, Hong Kong Park, Wan Chai Station]

▶ MORNING

Start off with a brisk stroll through **Hong Kong Park** (see p65), a green haven surrounded on all sides by thrusting towers of glass and concrete. Chances are you'll see several caparisoned couples awaiting their turn to be married at the Cotton Tree Drive Marriage Registry. Take time for a look through the Edward Youde Aviary, a spectacular creation of mesh arches replete with Southeast Asian birdlife.

Make your way down past Citibank's imposing black towers to Pacific Place for a coffee and some window-shopping. Keep heading towards the harbour and you will see to your right the elegant sweep of the **Convention and Exhibition Centre** (see p73). Enjoy the harbour panorama through soaring glass walls.

AFTERNOON

Return to Wan Chai for lunch. **Lockhart Road** (see p73) is as good a place as any. The sleazy joints are still slumbering, and there is decent pub grub, Thai, Mexican and Chinese food on offer (see p77).

Hennessy Road is the place to jump on a tram to Causeway Bay, due east of Wan Chai, or you may prefer to go one stop on the MTR. If you want to go shopping, take the Times Square exit, and start exploring from there. Then leave the crush and chaos behind with a leisurely afternoon stroll through **Victoria Park**, and perhaps a cocktail in Totts, the eyrie atop the **Excelsior** hotel.

See map on pp72–3 ←

Places to Shop

Sogo Japanese department store

① Sogo
MAP P6 ■ 555 Hennessy Rd, Causeway Bay
With a fine range of mostly Japanese goods, Sogo is very popular among locals. Stock up on Japanese food in the basement supermarket.

② Aeon
MAP F5 ■ Kornhill Plaza, 2 Kornhill Rd, Quarry Bay
One of Japan's biggest department-store chains. Lower rents to the east of the island translate into cheaper fashion, food and household goods.

③ Eslite
MAP N6 ■ Hysan Place, 500 Hennessy Rd, Causeway Bay
The largest bookstore in town and the first overseas branch of the Taiwanese chain famous for 24-hour openings. It also stocks stationery, gadgets and music.

④ Lee Gardens
MAP Q6 ■ 33 Hysan Ave, Causeway Bay
Hermès, Ralph Lauren, Gucci, Christian Dior and Cartier all reside here; Lee Gardens is the one-stop shop for the well-heeled.

⑤ Mezzanine
MAP E5 ■ 13–15 Yik Yam St, Happy Valley
Fashion designer to the stars Vivian Luk has opened her own couture store offering Oscar-style evening and especially bridal gowns.

⑥ D-mop
MAP N6 ■ Hysan Place, 500 Hennessy Rd, Causeway Bay
Cool multi-brand store carrying popular fashion-forward Japanese labels, such as moussy, SLY, and BLACK, as well as its own collection of clothing and accessories.

⑦ Spring Garden Lane
MAP N6 ■ Spring Garden Lane, Wan Chai
Head to this fun market for a bargain. Export-quality clothing is sold at rock-bottom prices.

⑧ Good Old Days
MAP P5 ■ 4/F World Trade Centre, Causeway Bay
A reminder of how quirky Hong Kong can be, this tiny store sells nothing but vintage classic watches.

⑨ Island Beverley
MAP Q5 ■ 1 Great George St, Causeway Bay
An arcane arcade stuffed with tiny boutiques featuring the creations of Japanese and Korean designers.

⑩ Fortress
MAP P6 ■ 7/F & 8/F Times Square, 1 Matheson St, Causeway Bay
This is the best chain to buy the latest electronics, sold at reasonable prices and with reliable guarantees.

Fortress electronics store

Places to Eat and Drink

PRICE CATEGORIES

For a three-course meal for one with half a bottle of wine and extra charges. Prices are quoted in Hong Kong dollars.

$ under $250 $$ $250–600 $$$ over $600

1 **Tasty Congee and Noodle Wantun Shop**

MAP Q7 ■ G/F, 21 King Kwong St, Happy Valley ■ 2838 3922 ■ $

For many this is the best place to go for beef fried noodles and piping-hot *congee* (rice porridge). The dim sum is also highly rated.

2 **Petrus**

MAP M6 ■ 56/F Island Shangri-La Hong Kong, Pacific Place, 88 Queensway, Admiralty ■ 2820 8590 ■ $$$

With two Michelin stars, Petrus serves contemporary French cuisine and boasts panoramic harbour views.

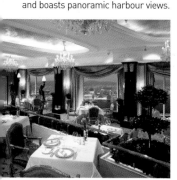

Elegant interior at Petrus

3 **22 Ships**

MAP N6 ■ 22 Ship St, Wan Chai ■ 2555 0722 ■ $$

One of Hong Kong's hottest tables for modern tapas creations by Jason Atherton. No reservations.

4 **Tai Lung Fung**

MAP N6 ■ 5 Hing Wan St, Wan Chai ■ 2572 0055 ■ $

This quirky local bar with an old-school Hong Kong decor attracts a young and artsy clientele.

5 **Yat Tung Heen**

MAP N5 ■ 2/F Great Eagle Centre, 23 Harbour Rd, Wan Chai ■ 2878 1212 ■ $$$

Drawing a strong local crowd, this award-winning Cantonese restaurant is famed for its soups and seafood dishes.

6 **American Restaurant**

MAP N6 ■ 20 Lockhart Rd ■ 2527 1000 ■ $$

Opened in the 1950s and still going strong. The name was a trick to attract US servicemen on leave during the Korean War. The Peking duck is superb.

7 **The Pawn**

MAP N6 ■ 62 Johnston Rd, Wan Chai ■ 2866 3444 ■ $$$

This popular old Chinese pawnbrokers, converted into a bar-restaurant, has atmosphere in spades. Serves modern European cuisine with a British twist by chef Tom Aikens.

8 **Bo Innovation**

MAP N6 ■ 2/F J Residence, 60 Johnston Rd, Wan Chai ■ 2850 8371 ■ $$$

Awarded three Michelin stars, this highly modern Chinese restaurant attracts a hip clientele.

9 **One Harbour Road**

MAP N5 ■ Grand Hyatt, 1 Harbour Rd, Wan Chai ■ 2584 7722 ■ Closed Sun ■ $$

For home-style Cantonese food at its most pure and subtle, with no fusion or foreign influences, head to One Harbour Road.

10 **Classified**

MAP Q7 ■ 13 Yuk Sau St, Happy Valley ■ 2857 3454 ■ $

Happy Valley has a host of trendy wine bars and eateries, including this outpost of the famous chain serving freshly-baked bread, artisan cheeses, gourmet coffee and specialist wines.

See map on pp72–3 ←

🔟 Hong Kong Island – South

Dolphin topiary, Ocean Park

Despite the slow creep of floodlit housing estates to the east and west, the south of Hong Kong Island (or "Southside" as everyone calls it) retains more than enough rugged coastline, wooded upland and sequestered beach to startle anyone whose preconception of Hong Kong was wholly urban. Traffic from the city passes through the Aberdeen Tunnel and enters a bright and shiny landscape of golf clubs, opulent homes and marinas. There is good swimming at Repulse and Deep Water bays, and even, at Big Wave Bay, some acceptable surf. Over at Stanley, stallholders set out their coral beads and antique opium pipes, while at isolated Shek O, media types snap up beachfront village houses. The Dragon's Back ridge, plunging down the southeast corner, offers some of the island's best walking.

AREA MAP OF HONG KONG ISLAND – SOUTH

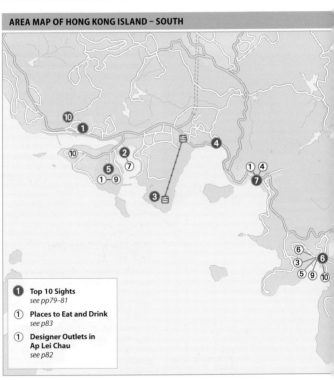

1 **Top 10 Sights**
see pp79–81

1 **Places to Eat and Drink**
see p83

1 **Designer Outlets in Ap Lei Chau**
see p82

1 Aberdeen Harbour
MAP E5

Residential blocks crowd Aberdeen's small, lovely harbour, which is still filled with high-prowed, wooden fishing boats, despite the fact that overfishing and pollution have decimated the Hong Kong fishing industry. Ignore the ugly town centre and instead photograph the tyre-festooned sampans, or walk to the busy wholesale fish market at the western end of the harbour and watch the catches being loaded onto trucks and vans.

2 Floating Restaurants
MAP E5

Also in Aberdeen Harbour are two giant floating restaurants, which are popular but garish, production-line eateries. The more famous, The Jumbo, is said to have served more than 30 million people. Prices are not especially attractive, nor are the culinary achievements (apart from Top Deck, see p83). Free ferries shuttle between these restaurants, and pushy sampan handlers also lie in wait for meandering tourists. Take one of these boats if you want a good view of the harbour. However, for quality seafood, head to Stanley or Repulse bay (see p80), or take a ferry from Aberdeen to Lamma Island (see p121).

The Jumbo floating restaurant

3 Ocean Park
MAP E5 ■ 3923 2323 ■ Open times vary. Check website for details ■ Adm ■ www.oceanpark.com.hk

This long-established theme park responded to the arrival of Disneyland on Lantau Island with a major refurbishment and a corresponding surge in popularity. There is more than enough to keep children and adults alike busy for a whole day. There are more than 30 permanent rides and animal attractions, ranging from rollercoaster rides to giant pandas and great aquatic displays, such as Atoll Reef, which recreates the habitats and sea life of a coral reef (see also p48).

4 Deep Water Bay
MAP E5

There's an almost Mediterranean air to the lovely beach and waterfront of Deep Water Bay, a popular place for beach lovers and the well-to-do who settle in the Bay's upmarket housing. The smallish beach is protected by lifeguards and a shark net, and the water is usually clean. As with most beaches in Hong Kong, it gets crowded in fine weather.

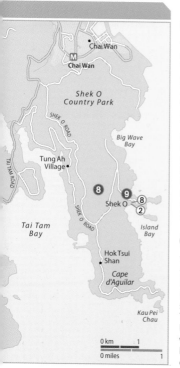

5 Ap Lei Chau
MAP E5

Supposedly the most densely populated island in the world, Ap Lei Chau (or Duck Tongue Island), opposite the Aberdeen waterfront, is crowded with a forest of high-rise apartment buildings. Bargain hunters may find a visit to the many discount outlets at the southern end of the island worthwhile (see p82). Close to the ferry pier are some small family businesses, boatyards and temples that have survived the modern developments.

6 Stanley

A former busy fishing village, Stanley was one of the largest towns on the island before the British arrived and placed a fort on its strategic peninsula. Relics from both eras remain, but Stanley's many excellent seafront restaurants and its extensive market are justifiably the main draws for visitors (see pp20–21).

Street sign

7 Repulse Bay
MAP F5

Another popular destination, Repulse Bay's beach is clean and well-tended, if sometimes over-crowded with thousands of visitors. Eating and drinking choices range from small cafés on the beach to The Verandah (see p83), a classy restaurant run by the same group as the Peninsula Hotel in Tsim Sha Tsui. Try afternoon tea here. The Hong Kong Life Guards Club at the far southern end of the beach is also worth a look for its scores of statues of gods and fabulous beasts.

Walkers on the Dragon's Back ridge

8 Dragon's Back
MAP F5

This 6-km (4-mile) walk looks daunting on the map, but the route along the gently ascending ridge of the Dragon's Back will mean not too much huffing and puffing for the reasonably fit. The reward is unbeatable views down to the craggy coastline of the D'Aguilar Peninsula, Big Wave Bay and genteel Shek O. At a gentle pace the walk should take about 3 hours, enough time to have built up a good appetite when you arrive in Shek O. Take plenty of water, especially in the summer.

Repulse Bay

Rocky coastline, Shek O

9 Shek O
MAP F5

Remote and undeveloped, the village of Shek O is worth the relatively lengthy train and bus ride necessary to reach it. The serenity is upset only at weekends by droves of sun worshippers heading for its lovely beach. A short walk to the small headland leads to striking rock formations, pounding waves and cooling South China Sea breezes. Surfing and body boarding are often viable on Big Wave Bay, a short walk or taxi ride north. Head to the Black Sheep (see p83), a lovely bar and Mediterranean-style restaurant, for a post-ramble beer and a bite to eat.

Steep steps at the Chinese Cemetery

10 Chinese Cemetery
MAP E5

Stretching away on the hill above Aberdeen, the Chinese Cemetery is a great place for taking photographs, both of the cemetery itself and of the harbour beneath. Negotiating the steep, seemingly endless steps is quite an undertaking, though, especially on a hot day.

A CIRCULAR TOUR

▶ **MORNING**

This circular tour of Hong Kong Island is perfectly feasible in one day if you start early.

From Central, jump on an Aberdeen-bound bus, alighting close to **Aberdeen harbour** (see p79). Haggle for a sampan harbour tour offered by one of the pushy touts on the waterfront. Don't expect any informative commentary from the driver. Keep a look out for Aberdeen's few remaining houseboats.

Avoid the production-line floating restaurants and opt instead for lunch at **Repulse Bay**, which is just a 15-minute bus ride away. Enjoy the beach and a swim, then eat either at one of the beach-front cafés or up-market **The Verandah** (see p83). Alternatively, head to the supermarket behind The Verandah and create your own picnic to eat on the beach.

AFTERNOON

Just a short hop further south along the coast, the lovely town of **Stanley** is certainly worth a visit. If you haven't yet eaten, the restaurants here are excellent, some with sea views. Lose a couple of hours browsing for clothes and souvenirs in **Stanley market**, though admittedly it is not one of Hong Kong's best or cheapest markets (see p59).

If you want to get some walking in, take a short bus or taxi ride to Tai Tam country park. A path leads through to Wong Nai Chung Gap, from where buses and taxis head back into the city.

See map on pp78–9 ←

Designer Outlets in Ap Lei Chau

 Horizon Plaza
MAP E5 ■ 2 Lee Wing St,
Ap Lei Chau

This shabby, high-rise building on the edge of the island of Ap Lei Chau (see p81) is home to a number of outlets for discount clothing, warehouse furniture, antiques and home furnishings. Start with an energizing coffee from the café in Tree on the top floor, before making your way down through the many stores. A taxi from Aberdeen is probably the simplest way to reach it.

② Joyce Warehouse
21/F Horizon Plaza

The extensive selection of clearance designer wear from the stores of Hong Kong chain Joyce are perhaps the main reward for struggling out to Horizon Plaza. You get discounts of 60 per cent on the likes of Armani.

③ Replay
19/F Horizon Plaza

A samples and warehouse shop from the high street brand with limited stocks of casual clothes, but great discounts, often around 80 per cent.

④ Inside
12/F Horizon Plaza

A modest warehouse outlet of a smart interior furnishings chain. There's a small range of clearance items at discounts that can be as high as 90 per cent.

⑤ The Birdcage
22/F Horizon Plaza

This one offers mostly original Chinese antiques and curios sourced by the owners of the quirky Birdcage shop on the mainland. Items range from portable antiques and collectables to furniture.

 i.t.
5/F Horizon Plaza

Off-season contemporary fashion lines by emerging Asian designers are sold here at discount prices.

Lane Crawford Outlet

⑦ Lane Crawford Outlet
25/F Horizon Plaza

Slow-moving items and old stock from Hong Kong's trendy department store are on sale here at lower than original prices.

⑧ Shambala
2/F Horizon Plaza

Antiques and vintage-style Western furniture with an Asian twist are crammed into Shambala's extensive store. After you're done shopping, stop by next door for some coffee at Pacific Coffee.

⑨ Indigo Living & Kids
6/F Horizon Plaza

Indigo does contemporary furniture and homewares with an Asian twist, with Indigo Kids the place for children's bedrooms and nursery furniture at a discount. They also offer design consultancy and furniture rental services.

⑩ Prada Outlet
2/F East Commercial Block,
Marina Square, South Horizons

Take your pick of last season's bags, accessories, shoes and clothes by the inimitable Italian designer Miuccia Prada. The minimalistic, stylish decor and layout ensure a true Prada experience.

Places to Eat and Drink

PRICE CATEGORIES
For a three-course meal for one with half a bottle of wine and extra charges. Prices are quoted in Hong Kong dollars.

$ under $250 $$ $250–600 $$$ over $600

1 The Verandah
MAP F5 ■ 109 Repulse Bay Rd, Repulse Bay ■ 2292 2822 ■ Closed Mon ■ $$

Indisputably Southside's premier venue, The Verandah, with its sea views and old colonial grandeur, is the place for big-budget romancing.

2 The Black Sheep
MAP F5 ■ 330 Shek O Rd, Shek O Village ■ 2809 2021 ■ $$

Stroll the quiet lanes of the bohemian enclave of Shek O on the southeast coast, and this veggie-friendly, hip café beckons.

3 Pickled Pelican
MAP F6 ■ 90 Stanley Main St, Stanley ■ 2813 4313 ■ $$

Reliable, tasty English pub food is served with speciality beers and a wide choice of Scotch whiskies here.

Tables in the street, Pickled Pelican

4 Spices
MAP F5 ■ G/F The Arcade, 109 Repulse Bay Rd, Repulse Bay ■ 2292 2821 ■ $$

One of the best places for alfresco dining in Hong Kong, Spices serves well-executed Thai and Indian curries in a lush garden setting. It offers a relaxed atmosphere and good service.

5 The Boathouse
MAP F6 ■ 88 Main St, Stanley ■ 2813 4467 ■ $$

Service could be better, but this is remedied by sitting upstairs or at the pavement tables with views out to sea, eating the contemporary European and North American cuisine.

6 Mijas
MAP F6 ■ 102 Murray House, Stanley Plaza ■ 2899 0858 ■ $$

End a satisfying day in Stanley at this atmospheric Spanish restaurant. Romantics will gravitate towards the balcony tables at sunset.

7 Top Deck
MAP E5 ■ Top Floor, Jumbo Kingdom, Shum Wan Pier Drive, Aberdeen ■ 2552 3331 ■ $$

Residents usually avoid the floating restaurants as most of them are tourist traps, but the revamp of Jumbo's top floor has brought the crowds back. The seafood buffet is excellent *(see p55)*.

8 Happy Garden
MAP F5 ■ 786 Shek O Village ■ 2809 4165 ■ $

Long running cheap-and-cheerful Thai canteen, just off Shek O's beach. Excellent *pad thai* and satay.

9 Smuggler's Inn
MAP F6 ■ 90A Stanley Main St ■ 2813 8852 ■ $

Stanley's gentrification has thankfully bypassed the Smuggler's Inn, which is a relic of the days when British soldiers from Stanley Fort blew half their wages here.

10 Lucy's
MAP F6 ■ 64 Stanley Main St ■ 2813 9055 ■ $$

Perennially popular venue for bistro-style nosh, with Mediterranean influences. There is a relaxed vibe and standards are consistently above par; a good choice for a light lunch or Sunday brunch.

See map on pp78–9

TOP10 Tsim Sha Tsui

On one level, Tsim Sha Tsui (universally truncated to "TST" in a merciful gesture to non-Cantonese speakers) is still a parody of a tourist quarter in an Asian port: its tailors and camera salesmen do not suffer fools, and its hostess bars are the scene of many a ruinous round of drinks. But there is also much more to Tsim Sha Tsui than that. There is a profusion of world-class cultural venues, galleries and museums, such as the Museum of History and the

Science Museum. There are hotels – the Langham, the Peninsula, the InterContinental – of jaw-dropping luxury. And every product and service the human mind can conceive of can be found in the monolithic Harbour City shopping mall.

Exhibit at the Museum of History

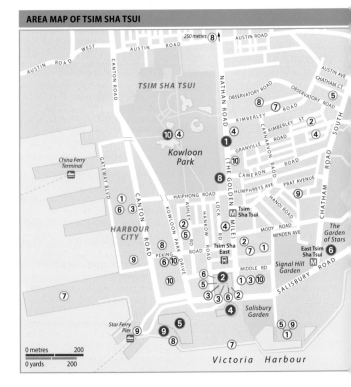

AREA MAP OF TSIM SHA TSUI

1 The Golden Mile
MAP N1–4

This strip that stretches up Nathan Road from the waterfront could be more accurately dubbed the "neon mile". It is less glitzy than Central and comprises mainly bars, restaurants, tailors, camera and electronic shops and the odd desultory topless bar. The crowds are so great that walking the Golden Mile becomes a major challenge.

2 The Peninsula Hotel
The last word in luxury service and accommodation. This venerable hotel sits like a proud old dowager, gazing sedately across at the vertiginous Hong Kong Island skyline. The cheapest rooms start where many other luxury hotels stop, although special offers sometimes apply. A night in the opulent

Neon signs on the Golden Mile

Peninsula suite will set you back almost the price of a small car. It boasts eight bars and restaurants, including the Philippe Starck-designed Felix and cognoscenti-favoured Gaddi's *(see p91)*. If you desire, you can swoop onto the roof by helicopter or be collected by Rolls-Royce *(see p148)*.

3 Museum of History
MAP P2 ▪ 100 Chatham Rd South ▪ 2724 9042 ▪ Open 10am–6pm Mon & Wed–Fri, 10am–7pm Sat & Sun ▪ Adm (free Wed)

This museum was built at a cost of almost HK$390 million, half of which was spent on its *pièce de résistance*, the Hong Kong Story, which attempts to chronicle the 400 million-odd years since Hong Kong coalesced from the primordial ooze. The story is told across eight galleries containing more than 4,000 exhibits, which vividly outline the natural environment, folk culture and historical development of Hong Kong.

4 Space Museum
MAP N4 ▪ Cultural Centre Complex, 10 Salisbury Rd ▪ 2721 0226 ▪ Open 10am–9pm Sat & Sun, 1–9pm Mon & Wed–Fri ▪ Closed for renovation till end of 2016 ▪ Adm (free Wed)

When you've had enough of history, come and peek into the future. This odd-looking dome in the heart of Tsim Sha Tsui includes an Omnimax theatre and interactive exhibits.

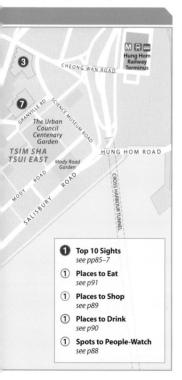

1 Top 10 Sights
see pp85–7

1 Places to Eat
see p91

1 Places to Shop
see p89

1 Places to Drink
see p90

1 Spots to People-Watch
see p88

The monolithic Cultural Centre with the clock tower in front

5 Cultural Centre

MAP M–N4 ■ 10 Salisbury Rd ■ 2734 2009 ■ Open 9am–11pm daily, Box office open 10am–9:30pm daily

With a peerless view beckoning across the water, the geniuses in charge decided to build the world's first windowless building, and covered it for good measure in public toilet-style pink tiles. Wander around and marvel at one of the great architectural debacles of the 20th century. That said, it hosts some good dance and theatre productions, as well as some free foyer performances.

6 The Garden of Stars

MAP N4 ■ Cnr of Salisbury Rd & Chatham Rd South ■ East Tsim Sha Tsui MTR Exit P1 ■ www.avenueofstars.com.hk

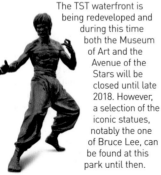

The TST waterfront is being redeveloped and during this time both the Museum of Art and the Avenue of the Stars will be closed until late 2018. However, a selection of the iconic statues, notably the one of Bruce Lee, can be found at this park until then.

Statue of Bruce Lee

7 Science Museum

MAP P3 ■ 2 Science Museum Rd ■ 2732 3232 ■ Open 10am–9pm Sat & Sun, 10am–7pm Mon–Wed & Fri ■ Adm (free Wed)

There are some fascinating interactive displays here if you don't mind fighting your way through the giggling, pushing throngs of schoolchildren. There are enough buttons to push, gadgets to grapple with and levers to tweak to satisfy even the most hard-to-please kids. Basic principles of science are explained in an entertaining manner, inviting hands-on exploration for both the young and young-at-heart.

8 Kowloon Mosque

MAP N3 ■ 105 Nathan Rd ■ 2724 0095 ■ Open 5am–10pm daily ■ Jumah (Friday) prayers at 1:15pm

When the muezzin calls the faithful to prayer, the Jamia Masjid Islamic Centre is where you'll find most of Hong Kong's Muslims. You can stop by for a look, but take your shoes off and be respectful. Entry to the inner part is not permitted unless you are a Muslim coming for prayer.

9 Clock Tower

MAP M4

The Kowloon-Canton Railway, which now ends at Hung Hom, used to finish at this clock tower, as did the rather more famous Orient Express (see also p18). From here,

CHUNKING MANSIONS

Following a major refit, this Hong Kong icon is no longer the sleazy, vermin-infested firetrap it used to be. Even so, the massive maze of a building remains infamous in many ways, not least for the fast-turnover shops, canteens and hustlers crowding its cavernous lobby, and the warren of cramped, budget accommodation filling the upper floors. But if you're after a dirt-cheap suitcase for those unplanned purchases, a discount phone-card or plug adaptor, or superb Indian food (try the restaurants on the 3rd floor), Chunking Mansions can deliver.

you can walk for more than a kilometre around the Tsim Sha Tsui waterfront and spot the occasional optimistic fisherman dangling a line in the harbour.

(10) Kowloon Park
MAP M–N3 ▪ Haiphong Rd
▪ Open 5am–midnight daily

While in Tsim Sha Tsui, if you feel one more whisper of "Copy watch? Tailor?" may provoke you to irrational violence, then venture through the park gates, find a well-shaded bench and watch the world go by. There's a big swimming pool (which is something of a gay cruising zone), an aviary and a pond with flamingos and other aquatic birdlife (see also p49).

Kowloon Park

A MORNING OUT

▶ MORNING

Catch the **Star Ferry** (see pp18–19) to Tsim Sha Tsui.

As you come in, check out the vast West Kowloon Reclamation site to the left, home of the shiny, silver **International Commerce Centre Tower** (see p38). The 118-floor monolith houses hotels, apartments and a viewing deck.

If you're still standing after the stampede to disembark (be wary of pyjama-clad old ladies), saunter past the old clock tower, pause to take in one of the world's most breathtaking views, then cross Salisbury Road and stop for tea at the **Peninsula Hotel** (see p85).

From here, brave the crush and bustle of the **Golden Mile** (see p85). Unless you want a new suit or dress, do not make eye contact with the legion of touts who have never heard the word "no". Walk straight by. They are merciless if they sense weakness.

AFTERNOON

When you've had enough of the smog-shrouded streets, hawkers and being jostled, cross Haiphong Road into **Kowloon Park**. There is plenty of space here to take a breather and do some serious people-watching.

You'll probably be getting peckish by now. Head back down Nathan Road to one of the excellent Indian restaurants in Chunking Mansions, or for something less hectic, the Peninsula Hotel has a host of culinary options.

See map on pp84–5

Spots to People-Watch

1 Tao Heung
MAP N3 ▪ Star Mansion,
3 Minden Rd ▪ 8300 8084 ▪ $$

Come here early and join the
Cantonese at their best – tucking
into a tasty, fresh and made-to-order
dim sum breakfast with their
families, or just sitting quietly with
a pot of tea and a newspaper.

Tao Heung

2 Chungking Mansions
The lobby is crowded with
African entrepreneurs, businessmen
from the Indian subcontinent and
nervous-looking backpackers queuing
for lifts up to their hostels *(see p87)*.

3 The Lobby at the Peninsula Hotel
Opulent Neo-Classical setting for
a rather fabulous afternoon tea
with the territory's smart set:
scones, cucumber sandwiches,
petit fours, a string quartet, the
works *(see pp85 & 148)*.

4 Kowloon Park
One of the best places in all
Hong Kong to visit at dawn, when
tai chi and martial arts practitioners
hone their skills among the
sculptures and fig trees *(see p87)*.

5 Felix
If the wallet won't stand up
to a meal, just take a drink at the
bar and watch everyone watching
everyone else *(see p91)*.

6 Harbour City
A people-watcher's paradise.
This massive labyrinth of inter-
connected malls has plenty of cafés
and benches from which to enjoy the
world passing by.

7 Waterfront Promenade
MAP M–N4 ▪ Salisbury Rd

Walking east from the Star Ferry,
you will meet tai chi adepts, culture
vultures and local ladies with their
tiny dogs. The promenade is very
popular for the harbour's Symphony
of Lights show, at 8pm daily.

8 The Langham Hotel
MAP M4 ▪ 8 Peking Rd ▪
2375 1133

Understated and elegant, the
Langham attracts similar clientele,
such as screen star Michelle Yeoh,
perhaps on her way to T'ang Court.

9 Star Ferry Pier
MAP M4

Inspiring place to take in Hong
Kong's bustle and watch the iconic
ferries and their passengers.

10 Heritage 1881
MAP M4 ▪ 2A Canton Rd

Heritage 1881 is the name given to
the super-swanky, revamped former
Hong Kong Marine Police head-
quarters. It features a boutique hotel,
bars and restaurants, and designer
shops attracting smart customers.

Boutiques at Heritage 1881

For a key to restaurant price ranges see p91

Places to Shop

Harbour City shopping mall

6 The Peninsula Hong Kong Arcade
MAP N4 ■ Salisbury Rd, Kowloon

A selection of fashionable designer boutiques, jewellers and bespoke tailors is located in the Peninsula Hotel (see pp85 & 148).

7 Toys 'R' Us
MAP M4 ■ Shop OTG23 G/F, Ocean Centre

Probably their biggest branch in Hong Kong. Kids will love it.

1 Harbour City
MAP M3–4 ■ Canton Rd

There are at least 700 shops in this vast agglomeration of malls stretching the length of Canton Road. It comprises the Ocean Terminal, Ocean Centre and Golden Gateway complexes.

2 Granville Road
MAP N3

Great for souvenir T-shirts, all manner of big-label knock-offs and factory seconds, as well as good-value clothing from chain stores like Bossini and Giordano.

3 Joyce
MAP N4 ■ G106 Gateway Arcade, Harbour City

Founder Joyce Ma is a Hong Kong fashion icon. Her flagship store is in Central, but the Harbour City outlet is also impressive.

4 Rise Commercial Building
MAP N3 ■ Cnr of Chatham Rd South & Granville Rd

It doesn't look much from outside, but inside this mall you will discover a trendsetter's utopia.

5 Beverley Commercial Centre
MAP N3 ■ 87–105 Chatham Rd South

The original beacon of cool in Tsim Sha Tsui, with floor after floor of mini-boutiques from local designers.

8 Chow Tai Fook
MAP N3 ■ Park Lane Shopper's Boulevard, 123 Nathan Rd

One of Hong Kong's major jewellery chains, home to a dazzling display of gold, silver, jewels and price tags.

Chow Tai Fook jewellery store

9 Fortress
MAP M4 ■ Shop 335–7, Level 3, Ocean Terminal

If you're after electronic goods and baffled by the sheer number of shops around TST, chain-store Fortress is a good bet. Other shops may advertise cheaper prices, but not all dealers are honest.

10 Sam's Tailor
MAP N3 ■ Burlington Arcade, 94 Nathan Rd

Portraits of former clients, including princes, presidents and pop stars, look on as the third generation of the Melwani family measures you for a well-priced, well-fitting suit that will be ready in two to three days.

See map on pp84–5

Places to Drink

The Lobby Lounge, with superb views across the harbour

 The Lobby Lounge
MAP N4 ■ 18 Salisbury Rd

Some of the best harbour views in Hong Kong are to be found in the bar of the superb Hotel InterContinental (see also p148). They more than make up for the price of the drinks.

2 Mes Amis
MAP N3 ■ G/F 15 Ashley Rd

A long list of wines by the glass and a full cocktail menu make this bar popular with visitors and locals alike. Daily specials and happy hours.

3 The Bar
MAP N4 ■ 1/F The Peninsula Hotel

This up-market watering hole serves as a delightful refuge from the Kowloon crowds – but prepare to pay through the nose for drinks.

4 Eyebar
MAP N4 ■ 30/F iSquare, 63 Nathan Rd

Uninterrupted Victoria Harbour views are highlighted with double-height windows and a telescope on the rooftop bar's terrace.

 Ned Kelly's Last Stand
MAP N3 ■ 11A Ashley Rd

This place has been here forever, as has the jazz band. Come here for an opportunity to get your feet tapping to tunes by the crustiest, most grizzled bunch of musicians this side of New Orleans.

 Aqua Spirit
MAP M4 ■ 29/F, 1 Peking Rd

Sit in a cubbyhole facing the window and sip a glass of bubbly as you watch the harbour light up.

 **Dada Bar & Lounge**
MAP N3 ■ 2/F De Luxe Manor, 39 Kimberley Rd

A gorgeous cocktail and wine bar, Dada Lounge is decorated in truly over-the-top style with Alice in Wonderland over-sized chairs, chandeliers and horse-head motifs.

8 Aqua Luna
MAP N4 ■ Tsim Sha Tsui Pier 1

Lie back on your day bed with a drink in hand on the ultimate harbour cruise; the *Aqua Luna* is the last traditional vessel to be built in Hong Kong. Daily sailings depart from Tsim Sha Tsui Pier 1 (see also p44).

9 Fatt's Place
MAP N3 ■ G/F 2 Hart Ave

This casual beer bar has a great selection of international ales and lagers by the bottle or on tap. Happy hour runs from 3 to 9pm daily.

 Sky Lounge
MAP N4 ■ 18/F Sheraton Hotel, 20 Nathan Rd

Another very comfortable, hotel-tower-top location from which to enjoy the nightly cross-harbour light show with a glass of something chilled to hand.

Places to Eat

 Oyster and Wine Bar
MAP N4 ▪ 18/F Sheraton Hotel,
20 Nathan Rd ▪ 2369 1111 ▪ $$$

A sublime view and oysters so fresh
they flinch when you squeeze a
lemon on them.

2 Felix
MAP N4 ▪ 28/F The Peninsula
Hotel ▪ 2696 6778 ▪ $$$

The cosmopolitan cuisine is fantastic,
the view is better and the bar is
crammed with the rich and famous.
Check out the interesting Philippe
Starck-designed urinals, where you
face wall-to-ceiling glass windows
and get a stunning view of Hong Kong.

3 Morton's of Chicago
MAP N4 ▪ 4/F Sheraton Hotel
▪ 2732 2343 ▪ $$$

A carnivore's paradise. Huge slabs of
cow aged and cooked to perfection.

 Cuisine, Cuisine
MAP N3 ▪ The Mira Hotel, 118
Nathan Rd ▪ 2315 5222 ▪ $$

Michelin-recommended Cantonese
cuisine fuses modern and traditional
in an elegant setting.

5 Nobu
MAP N4 ▪ 2/F Hotel
InterContinental, 18 Salisbury Rd
▪ 2313 2323 ▪ $$

Enjoy fine dining at one of the world's
most famous Japanese restaurants.

PRICE CATEGORIES
For a three-course meal for one with half
a bottle of wine and extra charges. Prices
are quoted in Hong Kong dollars.
....
$ under $250 $$ $250–600 $$$ over $600

 Gaddi's
MAP N4 ▪ 1/F The Peninsula
Hotel ▪ 2696 6763 ▪ $$$

Impeccable French cuisine,
irreproachable service and famous
patrons have earned Gaddi's its
reputation as one of Asia's finest
restaurants (see p55).

7 The Delhi Club
MAP N4 ▪ Floor 3, Block C,
Chungking Mansions ▪ 2368 1682 ▪ $

A low-key setting for some superb,
inexpensive, filling Indian curries,
this is a worthy reason to push
through the touts and crowds filling
Chungking Mansions' lobby.

8 Wildfire
MAP N3 ▪ 2 Knutsford Terrace
▪ 3690 1598 ▪ $$

A great place for pizza and pasta,
Wildfire has terrace seating at the
front and a rear courtyard garden.
It is a popular weekend brunch spot.
Branches also at the Peak, Causeway
Bay and Sai Wan Ho.

9 Spoon
MAP N4 ▪ Lobby of Hotel
InterContinental, 18 Salisbury Rd
▪ 2313 2323 ▪ $$$

Another superlative Michelin-starred
Alain Ducasse restaurant. Even the
550 spoons suspended from the
ceiling are unlikely to distract you
from the best French food in town.

10 Hutong
MAP M4 ▪ 28/F, 1 Peking Rd ▪
3428 8342 ▪ $$$

Updated Northern Chinese classics
are served in this theatrically lit
restaurant with magnificent views.

The bar at Nobu

See map on pp84–5 ←

TOP 10 Yau Ma Tei, Mong Kok and Prince Edward

Gritty, proletarian and utterly engrossing, Yau Ma Tei and Mong Kok provide a heady mix of karaoke bars, dodgy doorways and street markets before terminating in the more upscale apartments of Prince Edward. If Hong Kong has an emotional heartland, then it is these hectic streets, every paving slab the scene of some delicious hustle. Within living memory there were open fields here, but now all is uncompromising Cantonese ghetto. Come for some of Hong Kong's best shops, restaurants of rowdy authenticity and a sensuous barrage that will linger in your mind.

Door detail, Tin Hau Temple

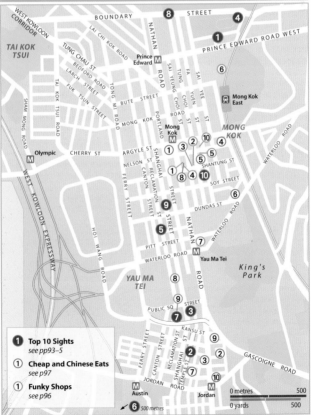

AREA MAP OF YAU MA TEI, MONG KOK AND PRINCE EDWARD

① **Top 10 Sights**
see pp93–5

① **Cheap and Chinese Eats**
see p97

① **Funky Shops**
see p96

0 metres 500
0 yards 500

↙ 6 500 metres

Stalls of colourful flowers at the Flower Market

1 Flower Market
Flower Market Rd

Near the Bird Garden is a vibrant flower market, at its brightest in the morning. The stalls and shops lining the entire length of Flower Market Road sell a wide variety of exotic flowers – a wonderfully colourful sight and a good place to take photographs. The market is especially exciting to visit during the Chinese New Year celebrations (see p60).

2 Temple Street Night Market

Visit the chaotic, crowded night market on Temple Street as much for the spectacle as for the shopping experience (see pp22–3).

3 Tin Hau Temple
MAP M1 ▪ 2385 0759
▪ Open 8am–5pm daily

The Tin Hau Temple in Yau Ma Tei is divided into three sections. Only one of these is actually devoted to Tin Hau, the sea goddess, who is Hong Kong's favourite deity and essentially its patron. Admittedly, it is neither the oldest nor the grandest temple in the territory, but it is pretty nonetheless. The other two sections are dedicated to Shing Wong, the god of the city, and To Tei, the god of the earth. Officially, no photography is allowed anywhere inside the temple. English-speaking visitors should head for a couple of stalls at the far end of the temple, where they can have their fortunes told in English.

4 Bird Garden
MAP E4 ▪ Yuen Po St

The pretty Bird Garden is where local folk, mostly elderly, take their birds to sing and get some fresh air with other birds. There's also a bird market (see p59) here selling sparrows, finches and songbirds in elegant little cages. Fresh bird food, in the form of live grasshoppers, is fed to the birds by their owners through the cage bars with chopsticks.

Bird cages in the Bird Garden

5 Reclamation Street Market
MAP E4

If you haven't seen a Hong Kong produce market in full swing, you could do worse than wander down Reclamation Street. The market sells predominantly fresh fruit and vegetables, and will provide some good photo opportunities. The squeamish, however, may want to avoid wandering inside the municipal wet-market building where livestock is freshly slaughtered and expertly eviscerated on the spot.

6 West Kowloon Reclamation
MAP L1–3

The reclaimed land of West Kowloon is a jumble of road intersections and messy building sites, as planners argue over exactly what will fill it. Rising 484 m (1,588 ft) over everything, the huge International Commerce Centre (see p38) opened in 2010 as the tallest building in Hong Kong, topping Two IFC. Its sky100 Observation Deck provides the highest indoor viewing platform in the city, with great harbour views.

International Commerce Centre

Jewellery stall, Jade Market

7 Jade Market
MAP M1 ■ Kansu St

The small, covered Jade Market is worth a quick forage even if you're not intending to buy any jade. Dozens of stalls sell jewellery, small animals (many representing characters from the Chinese zodiac) and beads in jade. There will be few bargains on sale, particularly to those without a knowledge of good jade, but there's plenty of cheap jade here if you just want to own some trinkets (see p59).

8 Boundary Street
MAP E4

History is visible in the ruler-straight line of Boundary Street, which marked the border between British Hong Kong and China between 1860 and 1898. The lower part of the Kowloon Peninsula was ceded (supposedly in perpetuity) by China to the British, who wanted extra land for army training and commerce. The British then became worried over water shortages and wanted yet more land to protect Hong Kong Island from the threat of bombardment from newly invented long-range artillery. In 1898 the border was moved again to include the entire New Territories, this time on a 99-year lease (see p36).

THE TRIADS

Overcrowded Mong Kok is the heartland of the Hong Kong triad gangs. The triads originated in 17th-century China as secret societies who tried to reinstall the Ming dynasty after the Manchus took over. Though they have been given a romantic image in literature and the cinema, the modern-day reality is of sleaze and slayings. Tourists are unlikely to be a target, however, so don't be put off visiting this exciting district.

9 Shanghai Street
MAP E4

The whole area around Shanghai and Reclamation streets is a traditional Chinese neighbourhood, if somewhat less vibrant and seedier than it once was. Interesting nooks and shops include funeral parlours, herbalists, health-tea shops, paper-kite shops and, at 21 Ning Po Street, a shop selling pickled snakes.

10 Ladies' Market
MAP E4

The term "ladies" is somewhat out of date, as there's plenty more than women's clothing here. The shopping area consists of three parallel streets: Fa Yuen Street, crammed mostly with sports goods and trainer shops; Tung Choi Street (the former ladies' market); and Sa Yeung Choi Street, specializing in consumer electronics. Market-stall prices are cheap, and shop prices are better than those on Hong Kong Island. The crowds here can be tiring, though, especially on hot days *(see p59)*.

Tung Choi Street, Ladies' Market

DOWN THE PENINSULA

▶ MORNING

Take the MTR to Prince Edward to start at the top of the Kowloon Peninsula, near the old Chinese border at **Boundary Street**. Take Exit B2 and head to the **Bird Garden** via the flower shops and stalls on **Flower Market Road** *(see p93)*. Testament to the Chinese love of exotic goldfish, the stalls at the top of Tung Choi Street sell a surprising variety of shapes and colours.

Cheap shops and market stalls abound a short walk away to the south on the streets below Argyle Street and east of Nathan Road. Pedestrians also abound – some 150,000 souls live in every square kilometre of this part of the Peninsula.

Crossing Nathan Road, head to the **Jade Market** for jewellery and figurines. If you want the best choice of jade, arrive before lunchtime because some of the stallholders pack up after this.

AFTERNOON

Take a breather in the small, pleasant square across the way and watch the world go by with the elderly locals, or peep inside the busy **Tin Hau Temple** *(see p93)*. Then break for a rough-and-ready cheap Chinese lunch in the covered canteens on the corner of Pak Hoi and Temple streets.

After lunch explore the produce stalls along **Reclamation Street** and the old Chinese district around **Shanghai Street**.

See map on p92

Funky Shops

1 King Wah Building
MAP E4 ■ 628 Nathan Rd
Head to this uncrowded mall for funky street clothing, great accessories, handbags and cool watches. There's genuine vintage denim and other 1970s and 1980s rarities, plus kitsch Japanese cartoon ephemera aplenty.

2 In's Point
MAP E4 ■ 530–538 Nathan Rd
Explore three floors of toy shops selling mostly Japanese anime figurines. There's also a Lego shop and one especially dedicated to legendary martial artist, Bruce Lee.

3 Izzue
MAP E4 ■ 26 Sai Yeung Choi St
High-end clothing chain for urban warriors and fashionistas in search of the perfect outfit for a night out.

4 Sony Pro Shops
MAP E4 ■ Sim City, Chung Kiu Commercial Building, 47–51 Shan Tung St
Head to the Sony Vaio, Walkman and PlayStation Pro shops for the latest audio and video gems among Sim City's computer shops.

5 Mongkok Computer Centre
MAP E4 ■ 8A Nelson St
The deals on computer hardware and software are not as good as those in Sham Shui Po, but this is convenient for a huge selection of games and accessories.

Mongkok Computer Centre

Sasa Cosmetics

6 Sasa Cosmetics
MAP E4 ■ MOKO, 193 Prince Edward Rd W, Mong Kok
Conveniently located outlet of an extensive Hong Kong chain selling cosmetics of every type at very low prices. Perfume is a bargain here.

7 Ban Fan Floriculture
MAP E4 ■ 28 Flower Market Rd
The porcelain and ceramic vases and wickerwork flower baskets are not likely to win awards for style or design, but the choice is impressive and the prices are reasonable.

8 Chan Chi Kee Cutlery
MAP M1 ■ 316–318 Shanghai St
Cheap, sturdy woks, steamers, choppers and pretty much everything else you might desire for the well-equipped kitchen.

9 Sandra's Pearls
MAP M1 ■ Jade Market stall, Kansu St
Reliable one-stop shop in the jade market for pearls, beads and jewellery of all sorts. Open between 11am and 4pm.

10 Sneaker Street
MAP E4 ■ Fa Yuen St
Sports enthusiasts will be in their element here. With a high concentration of sports shops, this is the place to be if you're looking for sports shoes, particularly rare or special editions.

Cheap and Chinese Eats

PRICE CATEGORIES
For a three-course meal for one with half a bottle of wine and extra charges. Prices are quoted in Hong Kong dollars.

$ under $250 $$ $250–600 $$$ over $600

1 Majesty Chinese Restaurant
MAP E4 ▪ 3/F Wu Sang House, 655 Nathan Rd ▪ 2397 3822 ▪ $

This bright, informal restaurant serves excellent and inexpensive dim sum breakfasts. Closes at 4pm.

2 Tai Ping Koon
MAP N2 ▪ 19–21 Mau Lam St ▪ 2384 3385 ▪ $$

Hong Kong's version of Western food at a branch of a century-old chain. Try the "Swiss" (sweet) sauce chicken wings or the roasted young pigeon.

3 Mui Chai Kee
MAP N2 ▪ G/F 120 Parkes St ▪ 2782 7301 ▪ No credit cards ▪ $

A great stop for fruit jellies and lotus-paste buns. The adventurous might try the bird's nest and egg tarts or frog's oviduct with coconut milk.

4 Chuen Cheung Kui
MAP E4 ▪ 33 Nelson St ▪ 2396 0672 ▪ $$

Hakka home-style cooking, which means salt-baked chicken and stewed belly pork with preserved greens are house specialities.

5 Saint's Alp Teahouse
MAP E4 ▪ 5 Jordan Rd ▪ 2374 0398 ▪ No credit cards ▪ $

Quirky snacks and an intriguing menu of teas in a modern Taiwan-style Chinese teahouse, which is one of an extensive chain.

6 Tim Ho Wan
MAP E4 ▪ G/F Olympian City 2, 18 Hoi Ting Rd, Tai Kok Tsui ▪ 2332 2896 ▪ $

Crowds queue up for the Michelin-star-rated lotus-leaf

Crowd outside Tim Ho Wan

rice packets, *cha siu* (barbecued pork) baked buns, persimmon cakes and *fun goh* (pork and shrimp) dumplings served here.

7 Ah Long Pakistan Halal Food
MAP N2 ▪ 95B Woosung St ▪ 2385 3382 ▪ No credit cards ▪ $$

A good bet if you fancy a decent spicy curry, although the surroundings aren't terribly pretty.

8 Fairwood
MAP E4 ▪ B/F King Wah Centre, 620–628 Nathan Rd ▪ 2302 1003 ▪ No credit cards ▪ $

Part of a large fast-food chain, this place serves Chinese and Western food.

9 The Lobby Lounge
MAP N1 ▪ 4/F The Eaton Hotel, 380 Nathan Rd ▪ 2710 1863 ▪ $$

Deserves a mention for its glass atrium, outdoor seating, terrific coffee and afternoon tea menus.

10 Light Vegetarian
MAP N2 ▪ 13 Jordan Rd ▪ 2384 2833 ▪ $

Cantonese mock-meat dishes on the à la carte menu, but the best deal is the ample lunchtime buffet, which includes desserts and a pot of tea.

See map on p92

🔟 New Kowloon

New Kowloon was home to the international airport of Hong Kong, Kai Tak, from 1925 until 1998. The site has not been allowed to lie fallow, with the former terminal having been converted into

the largest golf driving range in the world. In the neighbouring streets there are excellent budget dining options and seconds outlets, for this is where the locals go bargain-hunting. Cultural attractions can also be found to the north, in the Tang dynasty-style architecture of the Chi Lin Nunnery or in the joyful chaos of Wong Tai Sin Temple.

Colourful Wong Tai Sin Temple

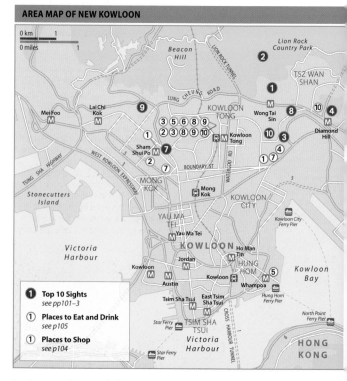

AREA MAP OF NEW KOWLOON

1 **Top 10 Sights**
see pp101–3

1 **Places to Eat and Drink**
see p105

1 **Places to Shop**
see p104

Previous pages Burning coils of incense on the ceiling of Man Mo Temple

1 Wong Tai Sin Temple
MAP E4 ■ Chuk Un ■ 2327 8141 ■ Open 7am–5:30pm daily

A noisy, colourful affair, Wong Tai Sin is always crowded and aswirl with incense smoke. Legend holds that Wong Tai Sin (originally known as Huang Chuping), who was born in Zhejiang province around AD 328, could see the future and make wishes come true. The temple opened in 1921, after a Taoist priest brought a sacred portrait of Huang to Hong Kong. The stylized architecture of the temple contrasts sharply with the surrounding concrete boxes. Worshippers from the three main Chinese religions – Taoism, Buddhism and Confucianism – flock here, not to mention tens of soothsayers hawking their services. Behind the temple is an ancient tomb that still baffles historians.

Lion Rock, resembling a lion's head

2 Lion Rock
MAP E4

One of the best places to view this fascinating landmark is, conveniently, from outside Wong Tai Sin temple. Find the open area near the fortune-tellers' stalls where you can look straight up at what, from this angle, resembles the head of a lion. Those feeling energetic may be tempted to scale its heights. Take lots of water, and be warned – the top section is not for the faint-hearted.

3 Kowloon Walled City Park
MAP E4

One of Hong Kong's most pictur-esque parks began life in 1847 as a Chinese fort. A legal oversight by the British left it under Chinese control after the New Territories were leased to Britain. It was levelled during World War II, and a ghetto called the Walled City sprang up in its place. This bizarre place was a magnet for Triads, drug deal-ers, heroin addicts and pornograph-ers (see p102). It was pulled down in 1992 and replaced by the park. A photography display in the alms-house by the entrance tells the story.

Bonsai, Kowloon Walled City Park

Pagoda in Nan Lian Garden, opposite Chi Lin Nunnery

4 Chi Lin Nunnery
MAP F4 ▪ Chi Lin Drive, Diamond Hill ▪ 2354 1735 ▪ Open 9am–4:30pm daily

It is said that not a single nail was used in the construction of this lavish replica of a Tang dynasty (AD 618–907) place of worship. The nunnery opened in 2000, funded by donations from wealthy families. The hall and side wings house impressive statues, including those of Sakyamuni Buddha and the Bodhisattva Guanyin. Do not miss the gorgeous, tranquil Nan Lian Garden opposite, which was similarly designed around Tang dynasty principles. Artfully arranged rocks, trees, bridges and wooden pavilions successfully conceal the garden's location in the middle of a busy traffic circle.

5 Lei Yue Mun
MAP F5

Once a fishing village, Lei Yue Mun translates as "carp gate", although the only fish you're likely to see nowadays are in the excellent seafood restaurants that line the waterfront. This is the closest point between Hong Kong Island and Kowloon, but don't be tempted to swim across the channel – if the pollution doesn't kill you, you'll be whisked away by the strong currents.

6 Oriental Golf City
MAP F4 ▪ Kai Tak Runway, Kai Fuk Rd ▪ 2522 2111 ▪ Open 7am–midnight daily ▪ Adm

This is, reputedly, the biggest driving range in the world, with more than 200 bays. Whack away to your heart's content – unless you're well-connected or seriously rich, this is as close as you'll get to a golf course in Hong Kong.

7 Apliu Street Flea Market
MAP E4 ▪ Apliu Street ▪ Open 11am–8pm

This huge street market is full of all sorts of strange junk and pirated goods. You'll feel like you're on another planet here – this is as "local" as Hong Kong gets. It includes perhaps the world's biggest collection of secondhand electrical appliances. Occasionally you can spot the odd retro turntable or radio, but most of it is rubbish (see p58).

THE MOST DENSELY POPULATED PLACE ON THE PLANET

More than 50,000 poor souls once inhabited the Kowloon Walled City (see p101), a place of few laws, but plenty of disease and criminality. In the 1950s the Triads moved in, and the lanes often ran red with blood. Before 1992 it was one of the few places left in Hong Kong with opium addicts puffing away on divans.

New Kowloon « 103

8 Fat Jong Temple
MAP E4 ■ 171–175 Shatin Pass Rd, Won Tai Sin ■ Open 10am–6:30pm Tue–Sun

Although it is one of the most famous Buddhist sites in Hong Kong, the Fat Jong Temple is little-visited by foreigners. Making it well worth the journey to see are the striking colour scheme (with red pillars standing out from the white walls), ornate decorations, magnificent Buddha sculptures and the superb vegetarian restaurant. The temple somehow manages to be busy and serene at the same time.

9 Lei Cheng Uk Tomb
MAP E4 ■ 41 Tonkin St, Sham Shui Po ■ Open 10am–6pm Fri–Wed

The Han burial tomb (AD 24–220) can barely be seen through a scratched sheet of Perspex. Still, it's one of Hong Kong's earliest surviving historical monuments housed within its own museum, so act suitably impressed.

10 Hau Wong Temple
MAP E4 ■ Junction Rd ■ Open 8am–5pm daily

Quaint and tiny, Hau Wong Temple is hardly worth a special trip, but take a look if you're in the area. It was built in the 1730s, however there seem to be a number of legends surrounding its origins. It's usually fairly quiet unless a festival is in full swing.

Entrance to tiny Hau Wong Temple

AN AFTERNOON IN NEW KOWLOON

▶ **AFTER LUNCH**

Catch the MTR to **Wong Tai Sin** (see p101) and brave the crowds of earnest worshippers at the temple. Some of the fortune-tellers in the nearby stalls speak English. Try to bargain them down to a third or quarter of the price given. Some use numbered sticks, others prefer curved bits of wood known as Buddha's lips.

If you're feeling fit, tackle **Lion Rock** (see p101). It's a demanding climb, but the views are superb. The steep inclines towards the top are for the stout of heart only. Take plenty of water.

A 10-minute taxi ride will take you to the **Kowloon Walled City Park** (see p101), Hong Kong's loveliest urban park. This tranquil green space contains eight different gardens.

LATE AFTERNOON

By late afternoon you should have worked up an appetite, so take a cab to the seafood restaurants on the waterfront at **Lei Yue Mun**. Watch the sun paint the sky-scrapers pink and orange as it sinks into the harbour, while you crack open crabs and munch on giant shrimps, all washed down with wine or an icy Tsing Tao beer.

With huge stone lions guarding its front door, one restaurant that is difficult to miss in Lei Yue Mun is **Kong Lung Seafood** (see p105). Here you can feast on a range of seafood dishes, including deep-roasted crab and steamed abalone with orange crust.

See map on pp100–1 ←

Places to Shop

1 **Golden Computer Arcade**
MAP E4 ■ 146–152 Fuk Wa St, Sham Shui Po
Spread across four chaotic floors is computer equipment available at good prices. Take care – many of the PS4 games and manga figurines available here are knock-offs.

2 Dragon Centre
MAP E4 ■ 37K Yen Chou St, cnr Cheung Sha Wan Rd, Sham Shui Po
Soaring glassy mall in the midst of Sham Shui Po's grime and dust. Good food hall, computer stuff and even an ice rink.

3 i.t.
MAP E4 ■ Shop LG2–02, Festival Walk, Kowloon Tong
This smart, minimalist outlet stocks stylish Japanese and American street clothes and accessories.

4 **Yuet Tung China Works**
MAP F4 ■ 3/F Kowloon Bay Industrial Centre, 15 Wang Hoi Rd, Kowloon Bay
One of the last places in Hong Kong still making Cantonese ceramics – tableware, decorative, personalized or monogrammed. Orders may take four weeks but shipping can be arranged.

5 Lancôme
MAP E4 ■ G18 Festival Walk, Kowloon Tong ■ 2265 8665
Ubiquitous luxury French cosmetics brand. Take your pick from the skin check-up or the 45-minute VIP consultation, or go straight for a 1-hour facial in a private cabin.

Lancôme

6 Page One
MAP E4 ■ Shop LG1–30, Festival Walk, Kowloon Tong
A massive branch of Hong Kong's great bookshop chain, this gets top marks for stacking books with the covers facing outwards, making them much easier to browse. It has a good coffee shop, too.

Page One bookshop

7 Yu Chau Street and Nam Cheong Street
MAP E4
The small shops that line these two streets sell an enormous range of laces, zippers, ribbons, beads and buttons – a wider choice than you might have imagined could exist.

8 BEYORG Beyond Organic
MAP E4 ■ Shop UG17, Festival Walk, Kowloon Tong
Organic, sweet-smelling goodies to pamper yourself with here. One of a number of branches across town.

9 Bang & Olufsen
MAP E4 ■ Shop G29, Festival Walk, Kowloon Tong
Audiophiles will drool over the sleek, Danish designs and crystal clarity from one of the world's most distinguished names in sound.

10 Millies
MAP E4 ■ 112 Level 1, Plaza Hollywood, Diamond Hill
One of the Hong Kong outlets of the largest retailer of women's shoes in China. It stocks a great range of shoes, particularly its own label.

Places to Eat and Drink

PRICE CATEGORIES
For a three-course meal for one with half a bottle of wine and extra charges. Prices are quoted in Hong Kong dollars.

$ under $250 $$ $250–600 $$$ over $600

1 Cambo Thai
MAP E4 ■ 25 Nga Tsin Long Rd, Kowloon City ■ 2716 7318 ■ $

Kowloon City is famous for its cheap and tasty Thai food. Be warned that you may need a cold beer to accompany the spicy beef salad.

2 agnès b. Délices
MAP E4 ■ Shop 20 Festival Walk, Kowloon Tong ■ 2265 8990 ■ $

The French fashion chain has opened a classy chocolate store and café. A heaven for chocoholics, it serves the sweetest treats in the area.

3 Exp
MAP E4 ■ Shop 23 Festival Walk, Kowloon Tong ■ 2265 8298 ■ $

A well-priced option serving Western and Asian favourites. Specializing in pizza, spaghetti and noodles, all with an interesting twist.

4 Chong Fat Chiu Chow Restaurant
MAP E4 ■ 60–62 South Wall Rd, Kowloon City ■ 2383 3114 ■ $

If you want to try traditional Chiu Chow seafood, this restaurant serves some of the best. Go for the tasty crab or goose dishes.

5 Wing Lai Yuen Sichuan Noodles
MAP F4 ■ 15–17 Fung Tak Road ■ 2726 3818 ■ $

Traditional Sichuan food in a plain setting. The dan dan noodles are the most delicious thing on the menu.

6 Kong Lung Seafood
MAP F4 ■ 62 Hoi Pong Rd West, Lei Yue Mun ■ 2775 1552 ■ $$

You can't miss this place – two huge stone lions guard the front door. This is a good bet for decent, fresh seafood. The deep-roasted crab and the steamed abalone with citrus reticulata rate highly.

7 Tso Choi Koon
MAP E4 ■ 17–19A Nga Tsin Wai Rd, Kowloon City ■ 2383 7170 ■ No credit cards ■ $

With a name that translates to "rough food", this is one for those prepared to take some culinary risks to experience the real Hong Kong. The adventurous dishes include sautéed pig's intestines and fried pig's brains.

8 Festive China
MAP E4 ■ Shop 29 Festival Walk, Kowloon Tong ■ 2180 8908 ■ $$

In fact, the festivities are fairly muted here, but the food is good. The northern-style Chinese cooking is served in the glossy dining room.

9 House of Canton
MAP E4 ■ Shop LG/F 40 Festival Walk, Kowloon Tong ■ 2265 7888 ■ $

The full range of Cantonese dishes, from abalone to an exhaustive assortment of dim sum snacks, is available here.

10 Amaroni's Little Italy
MAP E4 ■ Shop LG1–32 Festival Walk, Kowloon Tong ■ 2265 8818 ■ $$

Hong Kongers love Italian, and they have taken this place to their heart. Share the classic Italian dishes and make yourself at home.

Amaroni's Little Italy

See map on pp100–1

🔟 The New Territories

As a name, the New Territories is quite suggestive of frontier country – and in colonial times this was indeed the place where pith-helmeted sahibs went on tiger shoots, threw tennis parties and wrote memoirs. Today, much of the region is suburban rather than rural: more than a third of the population of Hong Kong lives here, in dormitory towns dotted across "the NT", as it is abbreviated by the locals. But to the north are the largest expanses of open country to be found in Hong Kong, including the important Mai Po Marsh, and there are centuries-old temples and settlements here, too. At the northern extremity of the New Territories is the border with "mainland" China.

Pagoda, Ten Thousand Buddhas Monastery

AREA MAP OF THE NEW TERRITORIES

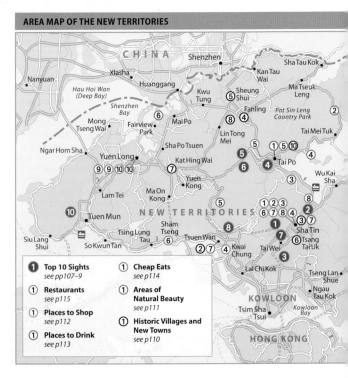

- ① Top 10 Sights
  see pp107–9
- ① Restaurants
  see p115
- ① Places to Shop
  see p112
- ① Places to Drink
  see p113
- ① Cheap Eats
  see p114
- ① Areas of Natural Beauty
  see p111
- ① Historic Villages and New Towns
  see p110

1 Ten Thousand Buddhas Monastery

MAP E3 ■ East Rail Line to Sha Tin, take north exit and follow signs ■ 2691 1067 ■ Open 9am–5:30pm daily

The Buddhas in question are stacked on shelves in the main hall of this hillside sanctuary at Pai Tau Tsuen, Sha Tin. In fact, there are more like 13,000 Buddha images now. The monastery comprises five temples, two pavilions and an elegant nine-storey pagoda. Take a deep breath before you enter the grounds – there are 400-odd steps to negotiate.

2 Sha Tin Racecourse

MAP F3 ■ Racecourse MTR ■ 2695 6223 ■ No children ■ www.sha-tin.com ■ Adm

Hong Kong's most famous horse-racing track is at Happy Valley on Hong Kong Island (see pp16–17), but the people who live in this part of the world are so mad about horseracing that they built a second racetrack in the New Territories. More than 85,000 punters have been known to pack Sha Tin's $500-million world-class track, where record-breaking sums are wagered on Saturday and Sunday afternoons between September and June. The racecourse was redeveloped for the 2008 Olympic Games so that the dressage and show jumping events could be held here.

Punters at Sha Tin Racecourse

3 Amah Rock

MAP E4 ■ East Rail Line to Tai Wai

This odd tower of rocks near Lion Rock Tunnel, when viewed from a certain angle, looks eerily like a woman with a baby on her back – hence the name. Legend holds that the amah's husband sailed overseas to find work, while she waited patiently for his return. When a storm sank his boat, she was so grief-stricken she turned to stone. An alternative interpretation is that the rock was created as an ancient phallic symbol.

Amah Rock

Sai Kung

PO TUNG RD
FUK MAN RD
MAN NIN ST
YI CHUN ST
HIRAM'S HWY

0 meters   200
0 yards   200

Tai Tan Hoi
Sai Kung West Country Park
Tai Wan
Shek Hang
Sai Kung East Country Park
Sai Kung
see inset above
Kausai Chau
Ngau mei Chau (Shelter Island)
Town Island
Basalt Island
Tseung Kwan O
Tai Wan Tau
Po Toi O
Tei Tong Tsui

0 kilometres   5
0 miles   5

4 Hong Kong Railway Museum

MAP E2 ▪ 13 Shung Tak St, Tai Po ▪ East Rail Line to Tai Po Market, then follow signs ▪ 2653 3455 ▪ Open 10am–6pm Mon, Wed–Sun

Tai Po's museum is not one of Hong Kong's best, but trainspotters will like it. Old coaches sit on tracks outside what used to be Tai Po Market Station. Inside is a tolerably interesting account of the city. Guided tours are also available.

Wishes left at Lam Tsuen Wishing Trees

5 Lam Tsuen Wishing Trees

MAP E2 ▪ Lam Tsuen Village ▪ MTR to Tai Po Market, then Bus 64 towards Kadoorie Farm and Kam Tin

People used to throw wishes, written on weighted strips of paper, from the branches of these trees. The practice was banned after the overloaded limbs broke off, so now wishes are pinnned on a nearby board instead.

6 Kadoorie Farm

MAP E2 ▪ Lam Kam Rd, Tai Po ▪ Bus 64K from Tai Po Market East Rail Line ▪ 2483 7200 ▪ Open 9:30am–5pm daily ▪ www.kfbg.org.hk ▪ Adm

Set up by local moguls Lord Lawrence and Sir Horace Kadoorie in 1951 to provide work for some 300,000 penniless refugees, Kadoorie Farm and Botanic Garden is now a centre for conservation and environmental awareness, promoting biodiversity in Hong Kong. Its 148 hectares (365 acres) of land include a deer haven and butterfly house.

7 Heritage Museum

Sha Tin's museum vies with the revamped Museum of History in Kowloon for the title of Hong Kong's best museum *(see pp26–7)*.

8 Yuen Yuen Institute

MAP E3 ▪ MTR to Tsuen Wan, then minibus 81 ▪ 2492 2220 ▪ Open 8:30am–5pm daily

This temple complex is popular with Buddhists, Confucianists and Taoists alike. It's usually full of worshippers, so be respectful. The main building is a replica of Beijing's Temple of Heaven. The notices outside carry the latest soothsayers' wisdom on which signs in the Chinese horo-scope are set for an auspicious year. Try the tasty vegetarian food in the Institute's restaurant.

Yuen Yuen Institute

SAVING THE SANCTUARY

The New Territories' Mai Po Marsh (see p42) is a world-class site of ecological significance, with more than 90,000 birds stopping there on migratory routes each winter. Kingfishers, herons and cormorants abound, and the marsh is one of the last habitats for the near-extinct black-faced spoonbill and Saunders' gull (below). Hong Kong's premier birdwatchers' paradise has been the subject of fierce debate and hard-fought battles between staunch environmentalists and developers desperate for scarce new land. The environmentalists, fortunately, have the upper hand. The biggest danger is pollution and industrial waste seeping into the marsh from factories at nearby Deep Water Bay.

9 Tin Hau Temple

MAP G5 ■ Hang Hau MTR, then minibus 16 towards Po Toi O ■ Open 8am–5pm daily

At the far end of Clearwater Bay sits the oldest of Hong Kong's temples dedicated to the sea goddess Tin Hau. The descent to it through a patch of forest is eerily quiet. Inside the temple, spirals of incense drop ash onto models of fishing boats.

10 Tsing Shan Monastery

MAP B3 ■ Castle Peak, Tuen Mun ■ West Rail Line to Tuen Mun ■ Open 6am–6pm Mon–Sun

The 2-km (1-mile) walk from the nearby light railway station is hard, but this is a nice outing to relieve stress if the bustle of Hong Kong is getting to you. Suck in some fresh sea air and let the chanting of the monks soothe your soul.

A DAY IN THE NEW TERRITORIES

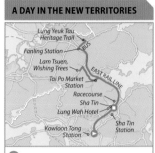

▶ MORNING

Take the MTR to Kowloon Tong, then switch to the East Rail Line train. Get off at Tai Po Market station, and take the 64 bus or a taxi to Lam Tsuen. This is home to the **Wishing Trees**. Buy a red paper strip from nearby stalls, write down your wish, then affix it to the adjacent boards.

Head back to the East Rail Line, and proceed to Fanling station. Take the 54K bus to Lung Yeuk Tau, start of the **Lung Yeuk Tau Heritage Trail** (see p110). This takes you through the five famous walled villages of the New Territories, which were built by ancient clans as safe havens from bandits. The walk takes a couple of hours, and provides a fascinating insight into what life once was like in these parts.

AFTERNOON

Take a bus or taxi back to the East Rail Line, and travel on to Sha Tin station. A short cab ride away is the Lung Wah Hotel, on 22 Ha Wo Che Street, which isn't a hotel any more, but a restaurant. This eating house has been going strong for more than 50 years, so they must be doing something right (though don't expect polite service).

If you are in Sha Tin on a weekend between September and June, head off to the **racecourse** (see p107) for an evening of thundering hooves.

On weekdays or out of the racing season, check out Sha Tin's excellent **places to shop** at New Town Plaza (see p112).

See map on pp106–7

Historic Villages and New Towns

Market stalls, selling fish straight off the boat, line the waterfront at Sai Kung

1 Sai Kung
MAP F3

Quaint fishing village turned expatriate haunt. Pubs with names like Steamers and the Duke of York are offset by old Chinese men playing mahjong in tiny cafés.

2 Tsuen Wan
MAP D3

This is the terminus of the MTR line and a perfect example of new town overcrowding. Worth a look just to see Hong Kong life at its bleakest.

3 Sha Tin
MAP E3

Less grim version of Tsuen Wan, with a massive shopping centre. Home to Hong Kong's second racetrack.

4 Fanling
MAP E2

Fanling's Tang Chung Ling ancestral hall belongs to the foremost clan in the New Territories. The Lung Yeuk Tau Heritage Trail is nearby.

5 Sheung Shui
MAP E1

Home to another of the main local clans, the Liu. From here, it's a quick cab ride to Lok Ma Chau, one of the border crossings with China, where the towering skyline of Shenzhen looms through the smog. This is the location of another ancestral hall.

6 Tsang Tai Uk
MAP E3

This stronghold of the Tsang clan dates back to 1848 and is built in typical Hakka style, with thick walls and a defensive tower in each corner. Dozens of families still live here.

7 Kam Tin
MAP C3

The name of this town means "brocade field", although little farming takes place here these days. Nearby are two traditional walled villages, Kat Hing Wai and Shui Tau.

8 Ping Kong
MAP E1

Off the beaten track, and therefore its walled village is less busy than others. The tiny Tin Hau Temple was featured in Jackie Chan's cult martial arts comedy *Project A*.

9 Tap Mun Chau
MAP H2 ■ Ferry
8:30am–6:30pm daily

One of the New Territories' best-kept secrets. Picturesque little island where villagers watch the world go by from their quaint homes.

10 Tai Po
MAP E2

Its market and Railway Museum are worth a quick look, before making your way to scenic Plover Cove.

Areas of Natural Beauty

Plover Cove
MAP F2

This isn't actually a cove, at least, not any more. In fact it's a massive reservoir which was created by building a dam across the mouth of the bay, then pumping all the seawater out and pumping in fresh water from China. Hike or bike the trails. Maps from HKTB.

Idyllic Plover Cove

Bride's Pool
MAP F2

Stunning waterfalls plunge into the pool amid the lush forest. Take a camera and wear sensible shoes.

Tai Po Kau
MAP F2

This forest reserve near the Chinese University is popular with serious birdwatchers and hikers.

San Mun Tsai
MAP F2

A charming fishing village perched between verdant hills and sparkling Plover Cove. Check out the local fisherfolks' floating homes with their dodgy wiring.

Tai Mo Shan
MAP E3

"Big fog-shrouded mountain" is the translation, although on many days the peak of Hong Kong's tallest mountain is visible. It reaches 957 m (3,139 ft) – quite a hike to the top, but superb views await the intrepid.

Turquoise waters of Tai Long Wan

Mai Po Marsh
MAP D2 ■ www.wwf.org.hk

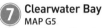
The marsh on the western edge of the New Territories is a bird sanctuary and nature reserve *(see p42)*.

Clearwater Bay
MAP G5

Various walks and beaches are on offer here. From Tai Au Mun, you can walk to the less than inspiringly named Clearwater Bay Beach One and Beach Two or Lung Ha Wan (Lobster Bay). There are occasional shark sightings during the summer, so beware before taking a swim.

Long Ke Wan
MAP H3

Relatively inaccessible little gem of a beach. Don't get too carried away with the view as you descend the vertiginous goat track, or you may find yourself at the bottom sooner than you intended.

Ma On Shan
MAP F3

The mountain's name means "saddle", a reference to its shape. Popular with hikers *(see p43)*.

Tai Long Wan
MAP H3

Hong Kong's finest beach, on the beautiful Sai Kung Peninsula. Take a good map and lots of water before setting off *(see pp28–9)*.

See map on pp106–7 ←

Places to Shop

1 IKEA
MAP F3 ▪ L6 HomeSquare, 138 Sha Tin Rural Committee Rd, Sha Tin

Even those who are not normally fans of the Swedish chain will find the wide array of made-in-China goods attractive.

2 Citylink Plaza
MAP E3 ▪ Sha Tin Station

This mall offers a wider range of more affordable brands than the nearby New Town Plaza.

3 New Town Plaza
MAP E3 ▪ 18–19 Sha Tin Centre Street, Sha Tin

This is the place to come to in Sha Tin for designer brands and high-end shopping. There are also cinemas and plenty of restaurants and a rose garden. An added attraction is Snoopy's World for kids, a small outdoor theme park featuring all the *Peanuts* characters.

4 Overjoy Porcelain Factory
MAP D3 ▪ 1/F Block B, Kwai Hing Industrial Building, 10 Chun Pin St, Kwai Chung ▪ 2487 0615

There are hundreds of patterns on offer, making this the perfect place to buy your dinner service.

5 Tai Po's Produce Markets
MAP E2 ▪ East Rail Line to Tai Po Market Station, then follow signs to temple

Tai Po is packed with atmospheric markets; those outside Fu Shin Street's Man Mo Temple are the best.

6 UNIQLO
MAP E3 ▪ Shop 225, 2/F New Town Plaza, Sha Tin

High-quality, but affordable Japanese clothing store. It has 18 branches all over Hong Kong.

Marks & Spencer

7 Marks & Spencer
MAP E3 ▪ Shop 428, 438, 4/F New Town Plaza, Sha Tin

Sensible shoes, comfortable underwear and comfort food for homesick Britons.

8 Bossini
MAP E3 ▪ A107–A108, Level 1 New Town Plaza, Sha Tin

Big branch of the cut-price chain store. Stock up on comfy cotton T-shirts, socks and khakis.

9 Hang Heung Bakery
MAP C2 ▪ 66 Castle Peak Rd, Yuen Long

Hong Kong's most popular baker of "wife cakes", a flaky pastry filled with red-bean paste. These traditional confections are *de rigueur* at Chinese wedding ceremonies.

10 Wing Wah Bakery
MAP C2 ▪ 86 Castle Peak Rd, Yuen Long

Hong Kong's premier purveyor of moon cakes *(see p56)*. These rich pastry treats are eaten during the Mid-Autumn festival. The egg yolks in the centre represent the full moon, although other fillings are available.

Stall at Tai Po's Produce Markets

Places to Drink

 After 5
MAP E2 ■ Shop A, 5 Mei Sun Ln, Tai Po ■ 2663 3551

The most popular of Tai Po's few Western-style bars, with cold beers from around the world. Steer clear of the overpriced wine list. If you're hungry, try the stewed pork hock.

2 Anthony's Ranch
MAP F3 ■ 28 Yi Chun St, Sai Kung ■ 2791 6113

Watch sports over an ice-cold beer while chewing on "Real Texas Smoke House" food such as barbecue ribs, brisket and pulled pork.

3 Steamers
MAP F3 ■ 66 Yi Chun Street, Sai Kung

A welcome little watering hole with a beer garden that serves pub grub including a full English breakfast.

4 Poets
MAP F3 ■ G/F 55 Yi Chun St, Sai Kung ■ 2791 7993

Don't let the name fool you. Loud discussions about the previous night's Premier League football matches are more likely than pompous declamations in iambic pentameter at this British-style pub.

5 The Boozer
MAP F3 ■ 57 Yi Chun St, Sai Kung

Much of Sai Kung's expatriate population can be found playing darts or watching sport on flat-screen TVs, while eating food brought in from the numerous neighbouring restaurants.

6 Bacco
MAP F3 ■ 21 Man Nin St, Sai Kung ■ 2574 7477

For a more sophisticated experience head to Bacco, where you can sample their extensive list of wines by the bottle or the glass. Upstairs is JoJo, an Indian restaurant run by the same management team.

7 Regal Riverside Hotel
MAP E3 ■ 34–36 Tai Chung Kiu Rd, Sha Tin

Three bars are on offer at this monolithic hotel – one lively and sports-oriented, the others more casual with great cocktail menus. All offer a respite from a hard day's shopping in New Town Plaza.

8 Tikitiki Bowling Bar
MAP F3 ■ 4/F, Centro, 1A Chui Tong Rd, Sai Kung

This is a perfect place for a family outing. The decor is stylish and it features a restaurant, two bars and ten bowling lanes. There's also a DJ, and live bands perform too.

Casa Sai Kung

9 Casa Sai Kung
MAP F3 ■ G/F Sui Yat, Hoi Pong Square, Sai Kung ■ 5594 0007

Head here for a modern take on tapas, washed down with craft beers, ciders and boutique wines. There is also live music and outside seating just steps from the waterfront.

10 Hebe One O One
MAP F3 ■ 112 Pak Sha Wan, Sai Kung ■ 2335 5515

There is a lovely colonial feel to this two-storied, balconied building, painted a soft, Mediterranean pink. Upstairs, the sea-view tables offer a perfect spot for enjoying a drink. Good for weekend brunches.

See map on pp106–7

Cheap Eats

Pepperoni's

1 Pepperoni's
MAP F3 ▪ 1592 Po Tung Rd, Sai Kung ▪ 2791 1738 ▪ $

One of the first decent Western-style restaurants in Sai Kung and still going strong. Huge servings and a relaxed ambience. There is excellent pizza, pasta, nachos, calamari and a good wine selection.

2 New Tak Kee Seafood Restaurant
MAP F3 ▪ 55 See Cheung St, Sai Kung ▪ 2792 0006 ▪ $

Buy your seafood from the market opposite or straight from the boats at the dock and simply pay the restaurant to cook it in your choice of Cantonese style.

3 Lardos Steak House
MAP F4 ▪ G/F 4B Hang Hau Village, Tseung Kwan O, Sai Kung ▪ 2719 8168 ▪ $$

Steaks are cooked to perfection by an owner who supplies Hong Kong's best hotels with their meat.

4 Sauce
MAP F3 ▪ 9 Sha Tsui Path, Sai Kung ▪ 2791 2348 ▪ $

In an intimate atmosphere, this excellent Italian restaurant serves home-made pasta. It also offers some modern European dishes.

5 Fuk Man Road
MAP F3 ▪ Sai Kung ▪ $

This road runs from the centre of town to the bus stations and is lined with noodle restaurants for the locals; dishes are usually served with brisket or offal so be careful what you order.

6 Yau Ley
MAP H4 ▪ High Island, Sai Kung ▪ No credit cards ▪ 2791 1822 (booking rec) ▪ www.yauleyseafood.com.hk ▪ $ (set menu only)

Fabulous seafood set menus in a little restaurant nestling in Sha Kiu village, reachable by road, hiking, ferry or the restaurant's boat.

7 Balcony
MAP D3 ▪ 3/F Kowloon Panda Hotel, 3 Tsuen Wah St, Tsuen Wan ▪ 2409 3226 ▪ $$

Stuff yourself with cut-price pasta from the set menus and marvel at the mediocre service.

8 AJ's Sri Lankan Cuisine
MAP F3 ▪ 14 Sai Kung Hoi Pong St ▪ 2792 2555 ▪ Closed Mon ▪ $

Light and tasty curries from the Indian Ocean can be enjoyed at Hong Kong's only Sri Lankan restaurant.

9 Honeymoon Dessert
MAP F3 ▪ 10A–C Po Tung Road, Sai Kung ▪ 2792 4991 ▪ $

Good-sized portions of various traditional desserts, with durian eaters segregated so as not to offend others with the strong smell of the fruit. Open until late.

10 Shaffi's Indian
MAP C2 ▪ 14 Fau Tsoi St, Yuen Long ▪ 2476 7885 ▪ $

This long-standing Indian diner is considered a Hong Kong institution. Founded in 1972, the restaurant would serve curries to the British soldiers at their Shek Kong base. It offers tasty and affordable lunchtime set menus.

Restaurants

PRICE CATEGORIES
For a three-course meal for one with half a bottle of wine (or equivalent meal) and extra charges.
....
$ under $250 ■ $$ $250–600 ■ $$$ over $600

1 Jaspa's
MAP F3 ■ 13 Sha Tsui Path, Sai Kung ■ 2792 6388 ■ $$

Good fusion food, friendly staff and lots of antipodean wines at reasonable prices. Part of a chain.

2 Tung Kee Seafood Restaurant
MAP F3 ■ 9/F, 96–102 Man Nin St, Sai Kung ■ 2792 7453 ■ $$

Point at what you want from the huge range of sea creatures swimming in waterfront tanks and haggle a bit. They bag it and cook it for you. One of the best seafood meals in Hong Kong.

3 Loaf On
MAP F3 ■ 49 Market St, Sai Kung ■ 2792 9966 ■ $$

Sai Kung's first Michelin-starred restaurant serves authentic Cantonese cuisine. Some locals claim the seafood dishes are the equal of any Hong Kong restaurant.

4 Royal Park Chinese
MAP E3 ■ 2/F Royal Park Hotel, 8 Pak Hok Ting St, Sha Tin ■ 2694 3939 ■ $

Classy Cantonese cooking – not an easy thing to find in Sha Tin. Specialities include dim sum, seafood and crispy chicken.

5 Tao Heung
MAP E2 ■ Shop A, Fuller Garden, 8 Chui Lok St, Tai Po ■ 8300 8127 ■ $

Bright, noisy dim sum restaurant in Tai Po, serving all the favourites: *har gau* prawn dumplings, *cheung fun* rice rolls and crispy *cha siu* pastries.

6 Sham Tseng Yue Kee Roasted Goose Restaurant
MAP D3 ■ 9 Sham Tseng San Tsuen, Sham Tseng ■ 2491 0105 ■ $$

Locals can't get enough of the stewed goose intestines, though the less exotic roast goose with salt and pepper is a better bet for tourists.

7 The Terrace
MAP F3 ■ 168 Che Keng Tuk Rd, Sai Kung ■ 2792 1436 ■ $$

A child-friendly restaurant that serves good Italian food. Its terrace, after which it is named, offers a lovely view over the marina.

8 Sha Tin 18
MAP E3 ■ 18 Chak Cheung St, Sha Tin ■ 3723 7932 ■ $$

In the Sha Tin Hyatt Regency Hotel, this stylish Chinese restaurant is especially good for southern Chinese seafood and meat dishes. There is a large outdoor terrace.

9 Tai Wing Wah
MAP C2 ■ 2–6 On Ning Rd, Yuen Long ■ 2476 9888 ■ $

Specializes in dim sum brunches and Poon Choi – a traditional New Territories casserole.

10 One Thirty-One
MAP F3 ■ 131 Tseng Tsau Village, Shap Sze Heung, Sai Kung ■ 2791 2684 ■ Closed Mon ■ $$$

Accessible by road or private boat, this restaurant serves fixed menus from its own organic farm. Book ahead.

One Thirty-One

See map on pp106–7

TOP 10 Outlying Islands

Hong Kong is often perceived as a city rather than an archipelago, but there are 260 islands in the group and, assuming you can haul yourself out of the downtown bars and boutiques, some of the territory's most sublime experiences await you here. Now that it is connected to the city by bridge, the largest of the islands, Lantau, is losing the quirky languor it once had, but the smaller islands offer plenty of compensation. From the narrow lanes of Cheung Chau to the outdoor raves of Lamma's Power Station Beach, Hong Kong's islands give you many opportunities to lose yourself.

Mui Wo beach, Lantau

① Lantau: Mui Wo
MAP C5 ■ Ferries from Hong Kong Island

Silvermine Bay, as the British named Mui Wo, is a good starting point from which to explore Lantau, though not the island's most beautiful spot. Most of the restaurants and bars, plus a supermarket, are around the corner from the ferry pier. There is also a beach 5 minutes' walk away. Enjoy a beer or stock up for a picnic before walking, cycling or beachcombing.

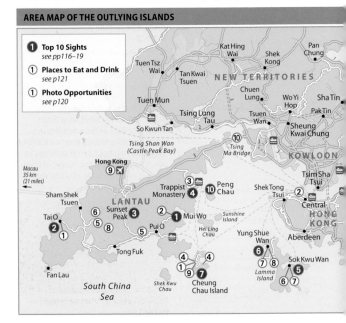

AREA MAP OF THE OUTLYING ISLANDS

- ① **Top 10 Sights**
  see pp116–19
- ① **Places to Eat and Drink**
  see p121
- ① **Photo Opportunities**
  see p120

② Lantau: Tai O
MAP A5

Lying on the far western coast of Lantau, the pretty village of Tai O is worth the long haul from downtown Hong Kong. Sitting in a tidal estuary, this is one of the last places in Hong Kong where you can see the traditional stilt housing of southern Chinese fishing villages. Some are as small as dolls' houses. For an authentic Hong Kong consumable, buy a jar of shrimp paste, a powerful type of fish sauce created by fermenting shrimp and spices in a barrel in the sun. It's actually much better than it sounds.

③ Lantau: Sunset Peak
MAP B5

For the reasonably fit, Sunset Peak offers the finest views on Lantau. The 934-m (3,063-ft) high mountain, Hong Kong's second highest, commands great views across Hong Kong, down onto the international airport, Po Lin Monastery and the lovely wooded valleys of this sparsely

The view from Sunset Peak, Lantau

inhabited terrain. Hardy souls stay at the nearby Youth Hostel and head up the peak for Hong Kong's most spectacular sunrise. Obviously all this only applies in clear conditions.

④ Lantau: Trappist Monastery
MAP C5

The chapel, next to a dilapidated old dairy farm, is open to visitors willing to observe the silence of the monastery. Apart from that, there's not much to see at the monastery itself, but it's a good excuse for a gentle woodland walk to or from Discovery Bay. The monastery is also served by a ferry pier, with infrequent *kaido* (small ferry) services to Discovery Bay and the island of Peng Chau *(see p119)*, which has many seafood restaurants.

An aerial view of Discovery Bay on Lantau

Seafood in Sok Kwu Wan

⑤ Lamma: Sok Kwu Wan
MAP E6 ▪ Regular ferries from Hong Kong Island

Don't expect many sights in Lamma's main area of development on the east coast of the island. Sok Kwu Wan is known mainly for its quarry and the wall-to-wall seafood restaurants along its harbour front. The seafood tanks are a sight in themselves, however, with some monster-sized fish and crustaceans. There's not much to differentiate the restaurants, although the standard is generally very good. Have a look at the pretty Tin Hau Temple at the end of the main street. The lovely 5-km (3-mile) circular walk to the sleepy, remote village and beach at Yung Shue Ha is recommended for the reasonably fit.

⑥ Lamma: Yung Shue Wan
MAP D5 ▪ Regular ferries from Hong Kong Island

The western coast of Lamma also has a harbour, with lots of bars and eating choices along the endearingly

LANTAU'S PINK DOLPHINS

The endangered dolphins (**below**) of the Pearl River Delta can usually be found at play near the coast of Lantau. A guided boat trip to see them is certainly worthwhile. Learn about the lives of these creatures and the threats they face, including pollution, overfishing and lethal boat propellers and hydrofoils. Tours leave at least four times a week *(see p49)*.

ramshackle main street of the village. Watch villagers, resident expats and fellow visitors wander by, before hitting the well-kept beach at Hung Shing Ye, which is a 20-minute walk to the southwest.

⑦ Cheung Chau Island
This former pirate haven retains much of its traditional character, from the small-scale shipyards at the harbour's edge to the old temples and shrines that dot its narrow alleys. With many of its inhabitants still being fishermen, it's a good destination for cheap seafood. There are also a couple of excellent beaches *(see pp30–31)*.

An aerial view of Cheung Chau's verdant coastline

8 Tap Mun
MAP H2 ■ Ferries from Wong Shek and Ma Liu Shui

To the north of the Sai Kung Peninsula, tiny Tap Mun, also known as "grass island", is another remote destination with only a couple of daily connections with the mainland. The rewards are striking rock formations, pounding seas, a herd of cattle and relative isolation. The island's Tin Hau Temple is surprisingly large and beautiful. Take a picnic, as there are few eating opportunities. Nor is there any accommodation on the island, so be sure to catch that last ferry.

A rock formation on Po Toi

9 Po Toi
MAP F6 ■ Ferry from Stanley or Aberdeen Tue, Thu, Sat, Sun & public hols

Getting to this barely inhabited outcrop of rock south of Hong Kong Island is most easily accomplished by taking the ferries that run from Stanley and Aberdeen. It's worth the effort for the secluded walks and spectacular cliff views over the South China Sea. Round off your day with a meal at the island's only restaurant, the Ming Kee (see p121).

10 Peng Chau
MAP C5 ■ Ferries from Hong Kong Island

This tiny island remains in many ways a traditional coastal community. You wander among its narrow alleys, tiny shops and temples to the gentle soundtrack of a distant game of mahjong or Cantonese opera leaking from an old radio. However, there's no beach, and few eating choices, though the seafood is cheap.

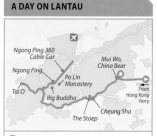

A DAY ON LANTAU

▶ **MORNING**

Make a reasonably early start for Lantau from the outlying islands ferry terminal on Hong Kong Island. After disembarking at **Mui Wo** (see p116), take the No.1 bus from outside the ferry pier to the old fishing village of **Tai O** (see p117) on the far northwestern coast.

Take in the sights and smells of this ancient settlement before catching the No. 21 bus to Ngong Ping for the **Big Buddha and Po Lin Monastery** (see pp32–3), or take a ride in the **Ngong Ping 360 Cable Car** (see p49).

 Have a vegetarian lunch at the monastery, or take a picnic. The area around Ngong Ping is great for gentle rambles with a view, as well as some serious hill climbing (Lantau Peak).

AFTERNOON

If time still permits, take the bus back towards Mui Wo, but jump out at the fantastic, clean and usually deserted beach at Cheung Sha (ask the driver to let you know when). Spend a relaxed afternoon paddling, swimming and sunbathing on this glorious stretch of golden sand.

Slake your afternoon thirst and tea-time hunger at **The Stoep** (see p121), which offers South African and Mediterranean food.

From here it's a short ride back into Mui Wo. Before catching the return ferry, squeeze in a drink at the **China Bear** (see p121), a convivial bar near the ferry pier.

See map on pp116–17

Photo Opportunities

1 Tai O Village, Lantau
The old fishing village on the remote northwest coast is the last settlement in the territory with a significant number of stilt houses, some almost as small as play houses (see p117).

2 Any Ferry Aft Deck
Gain some perspective on the dramatic skyline of the islands. The Star Ferries offer the best chance to capture the dramatic skyscrapers of central Hong Kong (see pp18–19).

3 Hatted Hakka Women
The large woven hats draped with a black cotton fringe come from the Hakka people, once a distinct ethnic group in the region. Many women wear these traditional hats around Hong Kong, though not all wearers are ethnic Hakka.

4 Cheung Chau Harbour
Handsome, high-prowed fishing boats, squat sampans and busy boatyards are just some of the sights (see pp30–31).

5 Big Buddha on Lantau
The dramatic setting of the island itself is worth a picture, let alone the mighty Buddha (see pp32–3).

Big Buddha statue on Lantau Island

6 Ngong Ping 360 Cable Car
MAP B5 ■ Lantau Island ■ 3666 0606 ■ Adm ■ www.np360.com.hk
The 25-minute cable-car ride provides one of the best photo opportunities in Hong Kong. From the car, you can see out over Lantau North Country Park, the South China Sea, Hong Kong International Airport, the Tung Chung Valley and the rest of the surrounding area (see p49).

7 Lamma Restaurants' Seafood Tanks
The restaurants display the subject of their menus alive and swimming in outdoor fish tanks. You'll see some edible leviathans here – from monster grouper fish to giant lobsters and an array of other fidgeting crustacea and teeming sea life (see p118).

8 View of Airport from Lantau Peak
MAP B5
Take a powerful lens on a clear day to get decent shots of the airport from Lantau Peak. The summit also offers terrific views down onto the monastery and surrounding country.

9 Hong Kong Airport Planespotters Platform
MAP B5
There's no official viewing area at the airport, so take a taxi or walk to the small hill (the only natural part of this man-made island) just opposite Tung Chung town. There's a footpath to the summit and its pagoda.

10 Tsing Ma Bridge Lookout Point
MAP D4
If big construction projects are your subjects of choice, then head to the free Airport Core Programme Exhibition Centre in Ting Kau. The viewing platform on the roof offers a great opportunity to photograph the elegant Tsing Ma and Ting Kau bridges.

Places to Eat and Drink

PRICE CATEGORIES

For a three-course meal for one with half a bottle of wine (or equivalent meal) and extra charges.

$ under $250 $$ $250–600 $$$ over $600

1 Tin Yin Dessert, Cheung Chau

MAP C6 ▪ 9 Tai Hing Tai Rd ▪ No credit cards ▪ Closed Mon ▪ $

Waterside canteen serving refreshing and unusual treats – try the sago with jelly and coconut milk.

China Bear, Lantau

2 China Bear, Lantau

MAP C5 ▪ G/F, Mui Wo Centre ▪ 2984 9720 ▪ No credit cards ▪ $

Missed the ferry? Never mind. Nip around the corner for the cheap lunch specials and 30 kinds of bottled and draught beer.

3 McSorley's Ale House, Lantau

MAP C4 ▪ Shop G11A, G/F D'Deck, Discovery Bay ▪ 2987 8280 ▪ $$

Popular with home-sick expats craving the taste of familiar dishes, such as fish and chips, pies, curries and hearty Sunday roasts. There's also Guinness and a choice of real ales to wash it all down.

4 Cheung Chau Windsurfing Centre Outdoor Café, Cheung Chau

MAP C6 ▪ 1 Hai Pak Rd, Cheung Chau ▪ 2981 8316 ▪ Open 1–6pm ▪ $

The "all-day" breakfast, snacks and mainly Western starters are good enough, but not as good as the view.

5 The Stoep, Lantau

MAP B6 ▪ 32 Lower Cheung Sha Village ▪ 2980 2699 ▪ No credit cards ▪ $

Mediterranean and South African fodder is served up on one of Lantau's loveliest beaches. Try the cold, Cape-style curried fish.

6 Rainbow Seafood, Lamma

MAP E6 ▪ 16–20 First Street, Sok Kwu Wan ▪ 2982 8100 ▪ $$

One of Lamma's better places for a full seafood splurge with a harbour view. Very popular with the locals.

7 Bookworm Café, Lamma

MAP D5 ▪ 79 Yung Shue Wan Main Street ▪ 2982 4838 ▪ No credit cards ▪ $

This place wears its organic, veggie and vegan heart on its sleeve, with its twee slogans to peace, love and tofu on its walls. Don't be put off. The service is friendly and the fresh food and fruit juices are exceptional.

8 Lamma Seaview Man Fung Seafood, Lamma

MAP D5 ▪ 5 Main St, Yung Shue Wan ▪ 2982 0719 ▪ $$$

Neither the best nor the cheapest seafood on Lamma, but the setting – overlooking the bay – is superb.

9 Cheung Kee, Cheung Chau

MAP C6 ▪ 83 Praya St ▪ 2981 8078 ▪ No credit cards ▪ $

Somewhat shabby premises, but the noodles are fresh and the dumplings and wontons are just right. There's no signage in English, but it's easy to find, just by the ferry pier – look for the sign "1959".

10 Ming Kee Seafood, Po Toi

MAP F6 ▪ Tai Wan ▪ 2849 7038 ▪ No credit cards ▪ $

Run by a restaurateur and his daughters, this is Po Toi's best restaurant. Reach it by junk or from Stanley and Aberdeen (see p119).

See map on pp116–7

ⓉⓄⓅ10 Macau

A-Ma Temple, near Avenida da República

Gambling is indisputably the main scene in Macau – it claims to earn more revenue from its 30-odd casinos than Las Vegas does – catering mainly to weekend visitors from Hong Kong and, increasingly, mainland China. However, the Portuguese also had 400 years of rich history here, leaving behind whole districts of cobbled lanes and impressive Iberian architecture. The indigenous cuisine, which fuses together Chinese and Portuguese elements, is another draw.

AREA MAP OF MACAU

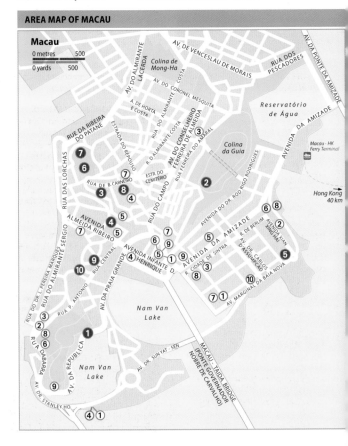

1 Avenida da República

The graceful boughs of banyan trees stretch over this elegant avenue, shading its candy-coloured pageant of colonial-era architecture. Unlike in Hong Kong, many of Macau's historic piles survive in excellent condition. At the gorgeous fort-turned-hotel of Pousada de São Tiago, the road becomes Rua de S. Tiago da Barra; follow it to the A-Ma Temple and the Maritime Museum *(see p126)*.

Guia Lighthouse, Macau's highest point

2 Guia Lighthouse

This most visible of Macau's landmarks has kept its lonely vigil on Guia Hill since 1638, its flashing beacon beckoning to everyone from Portuguese traders to ferocious pirates and marauding Dutch navy boats. Catch the cable car up the hill, take in the 360-degree panorama from Macau's highest point and enjoy a leisurely stroll back down.

3 Ruinas de São Paulo

Museum of Sacred Art: Open 9am–6pm daily; closed Tue pm

The façade and mosaic floor are all that remain of Macau's grandest church, perched atop a flight of stone steps and propped up by a viewing platform. In its heyday, it was hailed as the greatest monument to Christianity in the East. It caught fire during a typhoon in 1835, and only structural work in the early 1990s stopped the façade from crumbling. Behind it, a Portuguese influence is evident in many of the artifacts in the Museum of Sacred Art's rich collection.

Ilha da Taipa

See left

Macau Peninsula

Hong Kong 38 km

Ponte de Amizade

TAIPA ISLAND

Taipa Village

Macau

CHINA

Ilha da Taipa

COLOANE ISLAND

Reclaimed Land

Coloane Village

0 km   1
0 mile   1

Ruinas de São Paulo

The colourful Largo do Senado

4 Largo do Senado
Leal Senado: 163 Avenida Almeida Ribeiro. Open 9am–9pm Tue–Sun

Brightly painted Colonial buildings and slightly psychedelic paving make this square in the heart of Macau a favourite with photographers. At one end sits the Leal Senado, or Loyal Senate, now the seat of the municipal government but once the Portuguese headquarters. It was thus named because Macau refused to recognize the 17th-century Spanish occupation of Portugal.

5 Cultural Centre
Avenida Xian Xing Hai
■ **2870 0699** ■ **Open 11am–7pm daily**
■ **www.ccm.gov.mo**

This elegant building was designed and constructed in time for the December 1999 Handover to China. In fact, the actual ceremony took place behind the centre in a temporary structure designed to look like a giant Chinese lantern. The centre is the focal point for the Macau Arts Festival in March. The only mystery is why there is what appears to be a ski jump on the roof.

6 Protestant Cemetery
Open 8:30am–5:30pm daily

More interesting than it sounds – indeed, you might find yourself spending hours wandering this grave-dotted grove, reading inscriptions to plague-doomed sailors and colonial adventurers. Those at rest include painter George Chinnery (the Mandarin Oriental's bar in Hong Kong is named after him) and Robert Morrison, the first Protestant to venture to China in search of converts.

7 Camões Garden and Grotto
Praça de Luís de Camões
■ **Open 6am–10pm daily**

The author of the 16th-century Portuguese epic *The Lusiads* may never have visited Macau, but don't try telling the local Portuguese. Luís Vaz de Camões specialized in overblown, patriotic verse – a bust of him peers through the grotto's gloom. The gardens are popular with old men and their caged birds in the morning.

8 Fortaleza do Monte
Open 7am–7pm daily

These walls bounded the original Portuguese settlement in Macau – a well-stocked fort – which its inhabitants boasted could withstand years of siege. The sternest test came in 1622 when the Dutch, who had coveted Macau for years, made their move, only to be decisively beaten. The Portuguese military was based here up until 1966, at which point Portugal decided it was more politic to be administrators of Macau rather than gun-toting colonialists.

MACAU'S HISTORY

Macau was settled by the Portuguese in 1557 as a trading base and centre for Christianity. Colonial coats of arms can still be seen in Fortaleza do Monte **(below)**. Macau was nearly taken by the Dutch in 1622, and struggled to survive for the next 250 years. The Portuguese tried to re-establish power in the mid-19th century, annexing neighbouring islands Taipa and Coloane. It could never compete with Hong Kong, however, and gambling, opium and prostitution remained the main draws. Mao rejected a Portuguese attempt to return the enclave in the 1970s, but it was eventually handed back to China in 1999.

Façade of Dom Pedro V Theatre

⑨ Dom Pedro V Theatre
Largo de Santo Agostinho
■ **Macau Tourism Office for performance details: 2833 3000** ■ **Open 10am–6pm daily**

The first Western-style lyric theatre in the East, the Dom Pedro opened in 1858 designed in Neo-Classical style. It is still used to host performances. The hike up the hill is worth it for a look at a piece of theatrical history.

⑩ St Joseph's Seminary and Church
Rua do Seminario ■ **Church: 10am–5pm daily; Seminary: closed to the public**

The Jesuits constructed this chapel between 1746 and 1758, modelled on the Church of the Gesù in Rome. Its dedication plaque lists Portuguese King João V, Macau Bishop Hilario de St Rosa and Chinese Qing-dynasty Emperor Qian Long. The original bells still ring out, and fascinating Catholic artifacts can be found within.

Ornate altar, St Joseph's Seminary

Ruinas de São Paulo
Avenida Dr Sun Yat-Sen
Macau Tower
TAXI
Taipa Village
Cotai Strip
CHINA
TAXI
COLOANE ISLAND
Fernando's
Hac Sa Beach

▶ MORNING

Catch a taxi to the **Ruinas de São Paulo** *(see p123)* in the heart of Macau, pose for a picture on the steps in front, then lose yourself in the surrounding streets full of Chinese and antiques shops. The red lacquered trunks and cabinets, old teak tables and chairs are all cheaper than in Hong Kong's antiques shops.

When your feet start to protest, take a cab across the causeways to Coloane island and a lunch at **Fernando's** *(see p129)*. Get a large jug of piquant sangria in, then go for the fried chicken, garlic prawns, clams and sardines. The bread is hot and moreish, and the Portuguese salad is simplistic bliss.

AFTERNOON

Walk off lunch on **Hac Sa Beach** *(see p126)* or wobble your way to the minibus outside Fernando's and travel to Taipa village, with its picturesque houses and shops.

Then grab another taxi and head to the **Macau Tower** *(see p126)* for magnificent views of Macau and across the sea to Taipa, Coloane and the Cotai Strip. If you're feeling adventurous, you could try the Skywalk around the outer rim or even the bungee jump from the Observation Deck.

If you have the stamina, make your way to Avenida Dr Sun Yat Sen and its many bars for a night on the tiles or head to the swish bars and casinos of the Cotai Strip *(see p127)*.

See map on pp122–3

The Best of the Rest

Macau Tower, above Nam Van Lake

① Macau Tower
Nam Van Lakes area ▪ 2893 3339
Dominating Macau's skyline, this tower was built by casino mogul Dr Stanley Ho. At 338 m (1,107 ft), it just beats the Eiffel Tower and forms the centre of a convention and restaurant complex. The Skywalk and the glass-floored revolving restaurant are not for the faint of heart.

② Pousada de Coloane
Cheoc Van Praia, Coloane ▪ 2888 2143
Macau's first beachfront hotel is a top spot for a few cold drinks when the sun is shining.

③ Lou Lim Ieoc Garden
10 Estrada de Adolfo Loureiro ▪ 6am–9pm daily
Shady trees, benches and lotus ponds; a good place to unwind.

④ Macau Museum
Fortaleza do Monte ▪ 2835 7911 ▪ 10am–6pm. Closed Tue ▪ Adm
Good displays on the history and architecture of the region.

⑤ São Domingos
Largo do Domingos ▪ 10am–6pm daily
The pale yellow late 16th-century Spanish-style church towers over the Largo do Senado square. White ants forced extensive renovations in the mid-1990s. More than 300 sacred works of art are in the bell tower's museum.

⑥ A-Ma Temple
Rua do Almirante Sergio ▪ 7am–6pm daily
Images of junks decorate this pretty collection of halls dedicated to the patron deity of sailors, after whom the name "Macau" is derived.

⑦ Rua da Felicidade
The "street of happiness" once teemed with brothels, hence its somewhat ironically bestowed name. It's now a quaint, cobbled thoroughfare full of cheap eateries.

⑧ Maritime Museum
Largo do Pagode da Barra ▪ 2859 5481 ▪ 10am–6pm. Closed Tue ▪ Adm
This is the place to head if you are interested in learning about Macau's colourful seagoing past.

⑨ Pousada de São Tiago
Avenida da República ▪ 2837 8111
The beautiful hotel (see p154) overlooking the bay began life in the 17th century as a Portuguese fort hewn from the rock.

⑩ Hac Sa Beach
Coloane
Black-mineral-sand beach. Enjoy a stroll around the headland to the Grand Coloane Resort (see p154) for a drink.

Places to Gamble

Sands Cotai Central
Estrada do Istmo ■ 8113 6000
■ 24 hours

This resort combines 4 hotels, 20 dining options, shopping and gambling on a vast scale.

2 Sands
Largo de Monte Carlo 203
■ 2888 3388 ■ 24 hours

The first of the Vegas-style mega-casinos to arrive on the waterfront.

3 StarWorld Macau
Avenida da Amizade ■ 2838 3838 ■ 24 hours

This luxurious hotel has a distinctive Asian style and a large casino with an impressive LED wall. There are live shows every night.

4 City of Dreams
Estrada de Istmo, Cotai Strip
■ 8868 6688 ■ 24 hours

This opulent mega-casino is aimed at those with a penchant for ostentatious interiors and deluxe facilities.

Grand Lisboa
Avenida de Lisboa ■ 2828 3838
■ 24 hours

When casino mogul Dr Stanley Ho's original Lisboa hotel began to look dowdy, he built this extravagant party palace, complete with a giant casino and 15 restaurants, next door. Nowhere says "Macau bling" quite like this huge golden tower.

The Venetian
Estrada da Baía de N Senhora da Esperança, Taipa ■ 2882 8888
■ 24 hours

The full Las Vegas experience has been transported to the tropics. Live shows and big-brand shopping along air-conditioned streets provide a welcome break from gambling.

Indoor shopping at The Venetian

MGM Grand
Avenida Dr Sun Yat Sen, NAPE
■ 8802 8888 ■ 24 hours

An astonishing rippling façade, a fancy spa and a vast gambling hall in the style of a Portuguese town square can be found at MGM Grand.

Wynn
Rua Cidade de Sintra, NAPE
■ 2888 9966 ■ 24 hours

This is one of the most lavish casinos in Macau. The interior is decked out with floral carpets, extravagant chandeliers and plenty of colour.

9 Kam Pek Casino
51 Rua de Foshan ■ 24 hours

The loyal clientele of local punters here can be rude to tourists and flashy Hong Kongers. Prolonged eye contact with habitués is inadvisable.

10 Macau Jockey Club
Estrada Gov Albano da Oliveira, Taipa ■ 2882 0868 ■ Race meetings Wed or Thu & Sat–Sun ■ Adm

A bit less glamorous than its high-tech, cashed-up Hong Kong counterpart, but just as much fun.

Extravagant Grand Lisboa hotel

See map on pp122–3

Cafés, Bars and Clubs

Vida Rica Bar at the Mandarin Oriental Macau

① Vida Rica Bar
Mandarin Oriental Macau, Avenida Dr Sun Yat Sen
Great for watching Macau's movers and shakers, this extravagantly styled bar has an arty interior and fabulous harbour views.

② Bellini Lounge
Venetian Hotel, Estrada da Baía de North Senhora da Esperança, Cotai Strip
Tucked in a corner of The Venetian is this stylish bar. The surroundings may be plush, but the emphasis is on good live music, either from the two house bands, or from special guests. Check with the front desk for details of who is performing.

③ Club CUBIC
Level 2, City of Dreams, Cotai
Rather fabulous Hong Kong-owned club, with live DJs and cocktails at the weekend. A good place for celebrity-spotting.

④ 360 Café
60/F Macau Tower, Lago San Vai
This revolving bar, restaurant and café at the top of the Macau Tower boasts peerless views over the old city, the sea and islands.

⑤ Oskar's Bar
G/F Holiday Inn Hotel, Rua de Pequim
A mix of tourists and locals gather at this typical hotel-style bar, as well as the odd exponent of the world's oldest profession. Major sports events are shown on flat-screen TVs.

⑥ Vasco
2/F Grand Lapa Hotel, Avenida da Amizade
Enjoy tasty tapas-style fare and imaginative cocktails at Vasco. Best for a quiet evening drink.

⑦ CheChe Café
70A Rua Tomás Vieira
A low-key joint frequented by both locals and expats who come to socialize and have fun.

⑧ D2
Macau Fisherman's Wharf, Edf. New Orleans III
One of the city's liveliest dance clubs, D2 features a mix of music, with bar-top pole dancers at weekends.

⑨ Flame Bar
Level 2, Hard Rock Hotel, City of Dreams, Cotai
A fine selection of cocktails and an irrepressibly upscale party vibe feature at this lounge and club. Great fun if your credit card is up to it.

⑩ Casablanca Café
Av. Dr Sun Yat Sen
There's a pool table, lots of red velvet and posters recalling the famous film. Enjoy the in-house music, but resist the temptation to say "play it again, Sam" to the staff.

Places to Eat and Drink

1 Ming Ge Court
Langham Place Hotel, 638
Xingang Dong Rd, Haizhu ▪ 8916
3388 ▪ $$

The menu at Ming Ge Court features
high-class traditional Chinese
dishes, which are served in modern
yet culturally apt surroundings.

2 The Paddy Field
Central Plaza, 38 Huale Lu
▪ 8360 1379 ▪ $

One of the most popular expatriate
hangouts, this cheekily named
restaurant offers authentic,
traditional Irish fare. After a diet of
noodles, rack of lamb with mint
sauce can come as a shock.

3 Chuan Guo Yan Yi
4/F Nan Fang Securities
Bldg, 140–148 Tiyu Dong Lu
▪ 3887 9878 ▪ $

This restaurant gives an excellent
introduction to hot and spicy
Sichuan cuisine. Hotpot comes with
a yin/yang-style divider for those
unaccustomed to fiery foods.

4 Guangzhou
2 Wen Chang Nan Lu
▪ 8138 0388 ▪ $

The oldest and most famous
restaurant in the city, Guangzhou
is almost always busy. Guests can
choose from a massive menu of
Cantonese dishes.

5 Japan Fusion
2/F Metro Plaza, Tian He Bei
Lu 358–378 ▪ 3880 8118 ▪ $

In a city famed for its football-
field-sized restaurants, this is
one of the largest. A huge choice
of Japanese-Cantonese fusion
dishes is on offer.

Tang cu li ji – sweet-and-sour pork

6 Baiyun Xuan
Bayun Hotel, 367 Huanshi
Donglu ▪ 8333 3998 ▪ No credit cards
▪ $

A great opportunity to try – among
other Cantonese and Chaozhou
specialities – sweet-and-sour pork
(*tang cu li ji*) as it should be.

7 Fo World Sushishe
2–8 Niu Nai Chang Jie ▪ 8525
1300 ▪ $

Located south of the river, Fo World
Sushishe is considered one of the
best places to try Cantonese
vegetarian cuisine.

8 Orient Express
1 Shamian Bei Lu, Shamian
Island ▪ 8424 3590 ▪ $$

Enjoy good French cuisine in a luxury
train carriage or in the garden at this
Gallic-owned brasserie.

9 1920 Restaurant and Bar
183 Yang-jiang Zhong Lu
▪ 8333 6156 ▪ $

Expats and locals alike enjoy food with
a strong German influence. There's
also an outdoor terrace near the river.

10 G Bar
Grand Hyatt Guangzhou, 12
Zhujiang West Rd ▪ 8396 1234 ▪ $$

This impressive lounge is a stellar
spot for pre- or post-dinner drinks
while enjoying fine city views.

See map on pp134–5

Streetsmart

**Neon signs illuminating
Portland Street, Kowloon**

Getting To and Around Hong Kong

Arriving by Air

Hong Kong International Airport is on Chek Lap Kok, off Lantau Island, about 30 km northwest of downtown. Airport buses and taxis run around the clock, with the **MTR**'s Airport Express train (6am–12:45pm; HK$100) providing the fastest way to reach Kowloon and Central.

Macau International Airport sits on the east side of Taipa, about 5 km from the old city, handling traffic from China and Southeast Asia. Buses and taxis connect with the centre (15 min), and there's an adjacent ferry terminal for rapid transfers to Hong Kong (1 hr).

Shenzhen International Airport offers better-value flights to the rest of China compared to flying from Hong Kong. Buses connect the airport with **China Travel Service** branches in Kowloon (2–3 hr) and Hong Kong Island (2–3 hr).

Guangzhou Baiyun International Airport is one of China's busiest; it's 30 km from Guangzhou city, best reached by metro line number 3.

Hong Kong's national carrier is **Cathay Pacific**, offering direct flights to the US, Europe, UK, Australia, China and Southeast Asia.

Arriving by Train

Hong Kong's long-distance train station is **Hung Hom**, just east of Tsim Sha Tsui in Kowloon. Trains arriving from China terminate here, as do East Rail MTR services from the border at Shenzhen.

Guangzhou has multiple stations, but **Guangzhou East** (reached on the city's metro) is where to catch direct trains to Hung Hom. Shenzhen's main train station, where traffic arrives from across China, is at Lo Wu (Luo Hu), immediately across the border from Hong Kong. However, high-speed train services from China arrive at the Shenzhen North station and cross at the Futian border crossing. To reach Hong Kong from either, simply walk across the border and ride the MTR East Rail line to Hung Hom. Macau has no rail services.

Arriving by Bus

Hong Kong has no long-distance bus stations, but **China Travel Service** run a direct coach service to Shenzhen airport (2–3 hr) and a few hotels in Guangzhou (3–4 hr).

Shenzhen's biggest long-distance bus station is at Futian, handling traffic from all over China. There is a border crossing with Hong Kong here, linked to Hong Kong via the Futian MTR station. Macau also lacks a bus station.

Arriving by Ferry

The Hong Kong–Macau Ferry Terminal at Sheung Wan on Hong Kong Island, and the China Ferry Terminal on Canton Road, Tsim Sha Tsui, both offer fast catamaran services to Macau. Ferry transfers also operate between Hong Kong International Airport and Macau, Guangzhou and Shenzhen International Airport.

Macau's two seaports are the central **Jetfoil** terminal on Avenida da Amizade, and the Taipa Temporary Terminal, next to the airport on Taipa. Regular ferries run to Hong Kong, Guangzhou and Shenzhen.

Shenzhen's main port is at Shekou, about 10 km west of the Lo Wu border crossing with Hong Kong, though less from the Futian border crossing.

Getting Around by MTR

Hong Kong's MTR rail network has ten lines and a light-rail system, covering Hong Kong Island's north shore and Kowloon, the New Territories, the airport and northern Lantau Island. Services run daily 6am–midnight, and fares range from HK$5 to HK$50, depending on distance; the Airport Express costs HK$90 to HK$100 each way (multiple tickets are discounted). An **Octopus card** stored-value ticket gives a small discount on all fares.

Shenzhen and Guangzhou have extensive metro networks. There is no metro system in Macau.

Getting Around by Bus

Buses run across Hong Kong from 6am to midnight daily (with a few all-night services). Route itineraries are displayed at each stop, with numbers and destinations shown in Chinese and English at the front of the bus. Octopus cards are valid on all services.

Macau's buses (7am–11pm daily) are also comprehensive and very inexpensive; most routes cost just MOP$3–5 and you will need the exact change. Public buses in Shenzhen and Guangzhou are crowded and slow – it's better to take the metro.

Getting Around by Tram

Archaic double-decker trams rattle along Hong Kong Island's north shore between Kennedy Town and Shau Kei Wan, and cost about HK$2.30 a ride – pay the exact amount as you get off, or swipe your Octopus card. The Peak Tram is a bit of a misnomer; it's a funicular railway running from Central to the Peak Tower complex.

Getting Around by Taxi

Colour-coded taxis are everywhere in Hong Kong: red for the downtown, green in the New Territories and blue on Lantau Island. They are relatively good value for money at HK$20 to hire, then HK$1.50 per 200 m; expect to pay in excess of HK$350 from the airport. Excess luggage and the cross-harbour tunnels incur surcharges.

A taxi ride in Macau costs upwards of MOP$15, but the place is so small that fares rarely come to more than double this. Taxis are inexpensive in Guangzhou and Shenzhen; make sure that the driver uses the meter. Keep in mind the metro is usually quicker.

Getting Around by Ferry

Aside from the **Star Ferry** across Victoria Harbour, **First Ferries** run services to Lantau, Lamma and Cheung Chau islands around the clock from the outlying islands ferry terminal in Central. **Hong Kong and Kowloon Ferry** operates from Central to Lamma and Peng Chau, while **Fortune Ferry** serves Po Toi Island and Lamma from Hong Kong Island's south coast. Octopus cards are valid on most ferries.

Getting Around on Foot

Hundreds of kilometres of hiking trails weave across Hong Kong. Many are run by the **Agriculture, Fisheries and Conservation Department (AFCD)**.

DIRECTORY

AIRPORTS

Guangzhou Baiyun International Airport
w gbiac.net/en/byhome

Hong Kong International Airport
w hongkongairport.com

Macau International Airport
w macau-airport.com/en

Shenzhen International Airport
w eng.szairport.com

AIRLINES

Cathay Pacific
w cathaypacific.com

TRANSPORT DEPARTMENT

Transport Department
w td.gov.hk

TRAINS AND METROS

Guangzhou Metro
w gzmtr.com (Chinese only)

MTR
w mtr.com.hk

MTR Intercity
w it3.mtr.com.hk

Shenzhen Metro
w szmc.net

BUSES

China Travel Service
w ctshk.com

Hong Kong City Buses
w nwstbus.com.hk

FERRIES

First Ferries
w nwff.com.hk

Fortune Ferry
w fortuneferry.com.hk (Chinese only)

Hong Kong and Kowloon Ferry
w hkkf.com.hk

Jetfoil
w turbojet.com.hk/en

Star Ferry
w starferry.com.hk

OCTOPUS CARDS
w octopus.com.hk

TRAMS

North Shore
w hktramways.com

The Peak
w thepeak.com.hk

TAXIS
w taxihongkong.com

HIKING

Agriculture, Fisheries and Conservation Department (AFCD)
w afcd.gov.hk

Practical Information

Passports and Visas

Citizens of the US, Canada, Australia, New Zealand and most European countries only need a valid passport to enter Hong Kong for a stay of up to 90 days; British passport holders can stay 180 days. Your passport must be valid for at least one month after you intend to leave. Most visitors may stay in Macau for at least 30 days without a visa; and citizens of Schengen area EU states are allowed 90 days.

All foreign nationals require a visa to enter mainland China; these should be obtained through Chinese embassies and consulates in your own country beforehand, but visa regulations can change, so always check the latest requirements.

Five-day visas for Shenzhen (¥168) are available at Shekou Port, Huanggang Port and the Lo Wu (Luo Hu) crossing, but not at Futian. A 72-hour transit visa is available at Guangzhou airport for those arriving on international flights who have proof of onward travel to a third country (so you can't be on a round-trip from Hong Kong). Do not attempt to travel beyond the visa's permitted area, and check the latest information before travelling.

Customs Regulations and Immigration

Hong Kong and Macau are free ports and only levy customs duties on spirits and tobacco. In Hong Kong, visitors over 18 years old are allowed to import 1 litre of spirits of 30% ABV or higher (no limit on alcohol less than 30%); plus 25 g of tobacco products. Macau allows the duty-free import of 125 g of tobacco products and 1 litre of spirits.

Visitors to China can import 200 cigarettes or 20 cigars or 250 g of tobacco, plus 1.5 litres of alcoholic beverages over 12% ABV, and up to the equivalent of US$5000 in foreign currency. You cannot export anything of cultural importance (this may apply to antiques), nor any endangered animal or plant products.

Travel Safety Advice

Visitors can get up-to-date travel safety information from the Foreign and Commonwealth Office in the UK, the State Department in the US and the Department of Foreign Affairs and Trade in Australia.

Travel Insurance

Hong Kong, Macau and southern China are safe places, but visitors may encounter respiratory illnesses, traffic accidents and opportunistic theft. You are advised to take out comprehensive travel and health insurance.

Health

No vaccinations are required for Hong Kong, Macau or China, except for yellow fever if you're coming from an area where the disease is endemic. There are hospitals, clinics and dentists across the region with English-speaking staff. There is no free health care for visitors, so you'll have to recoup the costs for any consultations, treatment and prescriptions through your travel insurance policy.

Pollution is a major health issue. Tap water is best avoided, and locally caught seafood is unsafe to eat (most restaurants import theirs). Poor air quality, tropical humidity and crowded conditions contribute to the spread of respiratory complaints.

Seawater quality varies, and toxic algal blooms can make swimming ill-advised. Rare shark sightings off Hong Kong cause panic; stick to beaches that are netted and well patrolled.

Don't underestimate the stifling summer temperatures, when you should carry a bottle of water and avoid too much activity during the hottest part of the day. Wear cool, light, loose cotton clothing, with a hat. In winter, when temperatures can drop below 20 °C, bring a light sweater and a waterproof.

Personal Security

Keep a close hold on personal possessions, using a hotel safe if provided and not flashing valuable items around. Backpackers staying in dormitory accommodation may have their luggage robbed by unscrupulous fellow travellers. Don't wander the back streets at night; take a taxi. Women are unlikely to face sexual harassment, except perhaps in expat-heavy bars and clubs. Be careful crossing the road; traffic rules are ignored by many and accidents involving pedestrians are common.

Anyone caught eating or drinking on Hong Kong's spotless MTR system can expect to be heckled by irate fellow passengers, or even fined by the transport police.

A tough line is taken on illegal drugs; if convicted you can face time in prison, and China has executed foreign nationals for drug trafficking.

Hong Kong police wear blue uniforms; many speak English or will call for assistance if they don't. Chinese police also wear blue uniforms but are unlikely to be bilingual.

Currency and Banking

Local currencies are the Hong Kong dollar (HK$), the pataca (MOP$) in Macau, and the Chinese yuan (¥RMB). The ¥RMB is worth more than the HK$, which in turn is worth more than the MOP$. HK$ are accepted in Macau but ¥RMB are needed for mainland China.

As it's one of the world's financial hubs, you're rarely far away from a bank or an ATM in Hong Kong, and they are similarly common in Macau and China. Credit and debit cards are widely accepted by ATMs, and in hotels, restaurants and shops that see plenty of foreign custom, but at smaller businesses you'll need cash. Both banks and money exchangers (which are only plentiful in the downtown areas of Hong Kong) often give poor exchange rates compared with using an ATM – though check with your own bank about any transaction fees. In an emergency, money can be wired through local banks or **Western Union**.

DIRECTORY

CUSTOMS AND VISAS
Visas
w immd.gov.hk
w fsm.gov.mo/psp/eng/EDoN.html
w visaforchina.org
Customs
w customs.gov.hk
w customs.gov.mo
w english.customs.gov.cn

EMBASSIES AND CONSULATES
Australia
MAP N5 ■ 23/F, 25 Harbour Road, Wan Chai
w hongkong.china.embassy.gov.au
Canada
MAP L5 ■ 25 Westlands Road, Quarry Bay
w canadainternational.gc.ca/hong_kong
China
MAP N6 ■ 7/F, 26 Harbour Road, Wan Chai
w fmcoprc.gov.hk/chn
UK
MAP E5 ■ 1 Supreme Court Road, Admiralty
w gov.uk/government/world/hong-kong

US
MAP L6 ■ 26 Garden Road, Central w hongkong.usconsulate.gov

TRAVEL SAFETY ADVICE
Australia: Department of Foreign Affairs and Trade
w dfat.gov.au/smartraveller.gov.au
UK: Foreign and Commonwealth Office
w gov.uk/foreign-travel-advice
US: Department of State
w travel.state.gov

EMERGENCY SERVICES
Hong Kong & Macau fire, ambulance and police
C 999
24hr emergency hotline
C 139 24001705

HOSPITALS
Adventist
MAP E5 ■ Hospital, 40 Stubs Rd, Happy Valley
C 3651 8888
Global Doctor
136 Linhe Middle Rd, Tianhe, Guangzhou
C 020 38906699

Hospital Centre S. Januário
Estrada do Visconde de S. Januário, Macau
C 2831 3731
Island Emergency Station of Hospital Centre S. Januário
Macau University of Science and Technology, Avenida Wai Long, Taipa
C 2899 2230
Princess Margaret Hospital
MAP E4 ■ Lai King Hill Road, Lai Chi Kok, Kowloon
C 2990 1111
Queen Mary Hospital
MAP E5 ■ 102 Pok Fu Lam Road, Hong Kong Island
C 2255 3111
Shenzhen Hospital
University of Hong Kong Shenzhen Hospital, 1 Haiyuan 1st Road, Futian District
C 0755 86913333

MONEY
Exchange rates
w xe.com
Western Union
w westernunion.com.hk

Communications

Hong Kong's country code is 852; local phone numbers are eight digits long with no area codes. Calls within Hong Kong are free on private land-lines; many hotel lobbies have telephones for local use. Coin- or credit card-operated public phone boxes cost HK$1 minimum.

Several local companies sell local pay-as-you-go SIM cards, though none is better-value than the **Discover Hong Kong Tourist SIM Card**, which is available from the 1010 outlet at the airport, tourist offices and convenience stores across the city.

Hong Kong is well-connected to the Internet, with fast, free Wi-Fi available at the airport and most cafés, bars and public parks. Hong Kong Central Library, an enormous complex by Hong Kong Park in Causeway Bay, has both free Wi-Fi and hundreds of desktop terminals available, though these tend to get booked out by students.

Macau's country code is 853; local phone numbers are eight digits long, with no area codes, and the situation for landlines and mobiles is the same as in Hong Kong. Wi-Fi is not as widespread, but there are free terminals at the tourist office in Largo do Senado.

China's country code is 86; the city code is 0755 for Shenzhen, and 020 for Guangzhou. Most phone numbers are nine digits long. A Hong Kong SIM card may work here, if not, buy a Chinese one from any China Mobile shop or street kiosk, and top it up with a *chongzi ka* (prepaid card).

Free internet access is availiable via Wi-Fi in many cafés and some accommodation; hotel rooms are sometimes supplied with ADSL sockets too. Internet cafés are on the decline, and ID requirements make them difficult for foreigners to use. Expect some news and social media sites, such as Facebook and Twitter, to be blocked unless you have a VPN.

The Hong Kong postal service is rapid and efficient. Local mail takes one to two days. Zone 1 air mail (all of Asia except Japan) takes three to five days. Zone 2 (the rest of the world) takes five to seven days. The **General Post Office** operates a poste restante service.

The Chinese postal service is fairly fast and efficient, although overseas rates are pricey and sending parcels home always involves plenty of inspections and form-filling. Be warned that International Express Mail (EMS) is unreliable, despite offering registered delivery and online tracking services.

TV, Radio and Newspapers

English-language terrestrial TV channels include ATV World and TVB Pearl in Hong Kong, and CCTV 9 in China, offering a bland mix of news and entertainment.

RTHK is Hong Kong's publicly funded but editorially independent radio broadcaster. RTHK 3 has news, finance and current affairs; RTHK 4 plays Western and Chinese classical music; and RTHK 6 broadcasts BBC World Service programming.

Hong Kong's **South China Morning Post** provides conservative coverage of local, Chinese and world news, while the **Standard** tabloid offers a more irreverent spin. Over the border, the **China Daily** gives a sugar-coated view of China, but can be hard to find.

Local listings magazines include the bi-monthly **Time Out Hong Kong** and the free, weekly **HK Magazine**.

Opening Hours

Hong Kong's office hours are 9am–5pm Mon–Fri and 9am–12:30pm Sat. Most shops open daily but not usually before 10am, staying open until 7pm or later. Official hours in Macau are Mon–Fri 9am–1pm and 3pm–5pm, and 9am–1pm Sat. China's opening times are 9am–5pm Mon–Fri for banks and offices, with some opening through the weekend too, though with reduced services (banks might not offer foreign exchange then, for instance). Shops in China open early and close late.

Across the region, everything closes for the first three days of the Chinese New Year (late Jan or early Feb), with reduced hours for the rest of the two-week-long festival. Other days when you might find government offices and businesses shut are New Year's Day

(1 Jan), Qingming (4 or 5 Apr), May Day (1 May), the Dragon Boat Festival (late May or Jun), the Mid-Autumn Festival (late Sep) and National Day (1–3 Oct, China only).

Time difference

Hong Kong, Macau and China are 8 hours ahead of Greenwich Mean Time and 13 hours ahead of US Eastern Standard Time.

Electrical Appliances

Mains electricity in Hong Kong, Macau and China runs at 220V, 50Hz, so North American electrical devices will need converters. Plugs are British-style three square pins in Hong Kong but two round pins in Macau and China, though many Chinese plug sockets are universal. Adapters are sold at street stalls.

Driving Licence

Overseas driving licences are valid in Hong Kong for visitors staying for fewer than 12 months. Heavy traffic, expensive car rental and cheap public transport mean that there is little incentive to drive. Foreign licences are not valid in China.

Weather

Set just inside the tropics, Hong Kong, Macau and southern China share the same weather pattern. Summers (June–Sept) are torrid with temperatures hovering around 30 ºC (86 ºF) and typhoons that bring destructive winds and heavy rainfall; flights and ferries can be cancelled at short notice. Winters (Dec–March) are relatively cool and dry, with daytime temperatures sometimes as low as 15 ºC (59 ºF).

Information

The **Hong Kong Tourism Board** (HKTB) has three conveniently located branches open daily 8am–8pm: at the Star Ferry Terminal in Tsim Sha Tsui; near Exit F, Causeway Bay MTR station; and in a converted rail carriage outside the Peak Mall. Maps are available at bookshops.

The **Macau Government Tourist Office** is situated on the west side of Largo do Senado (daily 9am–6pm), at the Jetfoil Terminal (daily 9am–10pm) and in Hong Kong at the Macau Ferry Terminal, Sheung Wan (9am–6pm). They have a limited number of brochures and are useful for organizing discounted hotel bookings.

The China Travel Service in Hong Kong can handle visas, transport and accommodation bookings; once in China, your hotel is the best place to seek local information.

Disabled Travellers

Hong Kong is the only place in the region with a widespread understanding of disabled needs; the HKTB website has an informative "Accessible Hong Kong" section. They offer information about facilities in Macau, Shenzhen and Guangzhou, though these are limited.

Language

The Hong Kong region is primarily Cantonese-speaking. Mandarin Chinese is the official language of education and business, and is also widely understood. English is spoken and used on signage all over the city, though less so in the New Territories.

A decreasing number of people speak Portuguese in Macau. In Shenzhen and Guangzhou, street signs are in English, but you'll need some spoken Chinese or a phrasebook to get far on your own.

Shopping

Hong Kong has no sales taxes except on cars, cosmetics, alcohol and tobacco. However, there is a premium on style, so any big-brand fashion items are expensive. The advent of internet shopping also means that electronic gadgets are unlikely to be good value either. If you do spot a bargain, insist on an international warranty and be very careful not to be scammed; unscrupulous dealers along Nathan Road are notorious for switching the model they've shown you with an inferior, or faulty item.

Locally made clothing is good value in Hong Kong. Brands such as **Baleno** or **Giordano** offer smart-casual wear, and a clutch of long-established tailors can run up formal suits or dresses within a few days. For cheap clothing, try the markets at Sham Shui Po; for discounted designer wear head to the outlets on Ap Lei Chau (see p82).

Hollywood Road is where to find antiques and modern art, though these command high prices and any apparent bargains will be reproductions or fakes. For souvenir-quality items try Cat Street (see p59).

It's worth trying to haggle at small businesses, such as the many independent computer and electrical accessories stores, at the Temple Street Night Market (see pp22–3), and stores on Cat Street.

Shenzhen used to be a popular destination for bargain-conscious Hong Kongers, but nowadays prices have risen and it's not always a good place to shop. At the border, Luo Hu Commercial City sells just about everything, but is best for clothing; buy cut-price electronics at the SEG Computer Market, Futian district; and try the Dongmen district for curios, clothes and fabric.

Pirated gear, imitations and outright fakes are rife everywhere, so know your subject and bargain hard.

Eating and Drinking

Hong Kong is one of the best places in the world to eat, with restaurants on almost every corner offering everything from indigenous Cantonese and regional Chinese cooking to international cuisine. Cheapest are the chaa chan tengs ("tea canteens"), stalls at indoor markets, and local fast-food chains such as Fairwood and Tsui Wah, which serve one-dish rice or noodle dishes.

Barbecued pork (cha siu) and wonton noodle soup are Hong Kong's

signature dishes; many Cantonese restaurants also serve dim sum (yum cha) breakfasts, where you order a variety of small dumplings and pastries with Chinese tea. Lunchtime all-you-can-eat buffets are offered by many hotels, with the area around Central, SoHo and Lan Kwai Fong a hotbed of foreign cuisine, including Egyptian, British, Russian, French, Spanish and Vietnamese. Causeway Bay is the focus for Thai food, while Chungking Mansions (see p87) is famous for its good-value Indian restaurants.

Shenzhen's food is nothing special, but Guangzhou has some superb Cantonese restaurants, while Macanese cuisine fuses local Chinese and colonial Portuguese flavours.

Tea is the traditional Chinese beverage – both green and fermented – with dark bo lei (pu'er) the favourite accompaniment to a dim sum meal. Coffee was rarely drunk in the past, but globalization has brought a café culture.

Most of Hong Kong's bars offer long happy hours or promotions before a certain time of evening. Avoid the hostess bars in Wan Chai and Tsim Sha Tsui, unless you want to pay steep cover charges on top of your already expensive drinks.

Trips and Tours

The **Hong Kong Tourist Board** offers a raft of good-value options, from guided tours of Kowloon's markets to courses in tai chi and excursions to traditional villages. The

China Travel Service (CTS) can organize visas, tours and packages to Macau and mainland China. **Splendid Tours** specialize in excursions around Hong Kong, Macau, Shenzhen and Guangzhou. Package coach tours covering the region can be booked through **Gray Line Tours**. Explore the coast with day and night **harbour cruises**, some with drinks, either on refitted ferries or aboard the **Aqua Luna** wooden junk. Various companies offer **junks** for private charter around Hong Kong's many islands. **Walking tours** for all levels explore Hong Kong's architecture, heritage, wildlife and countryside.

Where to Stay

With plenty of accommodation in Hong Kong, there is always somewhere to stay at short notice, but to save money you'll need to book well in advance, especially around holidays and major sporting events. Always expect high prices for what you get, and to pay a premium for space. At the budget end of things, rooms are barely big enough for the bed. Breakfast is seldom included except at top-of-the-range places. A 3 per cent government tax and a 10 per cent service charge will be added to the bill at all but the cheapest guesthouses.

There are two central **YHA** youth hostels in Hong Kong, which have dorms, self-catering kitchens and a few private rooms.

Hong Kong has whole apartment buildings – such as the notorious **Chungking Mansions** in Tsim Sha Tsui – filled with private hostels and guesthouses. Though the buildings themselves might be intimidating, many of the places to stay are well-run and offer good-value dorms, doubles and even basic en suites, though conditions are extremely cramped.

Slightly better rooms, facilities and higher prices are offered by various church and international organizations such as the **YMCA** and Scouts.

Hotels range from fairly basic business models and quirky boutique brands up to some of the world's best, featuring stunning harbour views and prices to match.

Macau has a good range of hotels including some staggeringly opulent casino-resorts, but very few real budget options. Prices are lower than in Hong Kong, and rooms larger. Shenzhen's options are largely business-oriented, well-equipped and no more expensive than a budget guesthouse in Hong Kong, if you stick to the domestic chains.

DIRECTORY

SHOPPING
Baleno
🔲 baleno.com
Giordano
🔲 giordano.com
Hong Kong
🔲 discoverhongkong.com/eng/shop
Shenzhen
🔲 shenzhenshopper.com

EATING AND DRINKING
Hong Kong Clubbing
🔲 hkclubbing.com
Open Rice Restaurant Reviews
🔲 openrice.com/en/hongkong

TRIPS AND TOURS
China Travel Service
🔲 ctshk.com

Gray Line Tours
🔲 grayline.com.hk
Guided walks
🔲 walkhongkong.com
🔲 jasonwordie.com
Harbour cruises
🔲 starferry.com.hk/harbourtour
🔲 aqualuna.com.hk
Hong Kong Tourist Board
🔲 discoverhongkong.com
Junk hire
🔲 islandjunks.com.hk
🔲 saffron-cruises.com
Splendid Tours
🔲 splendid.hk

ACCOMMODATION
Asia Rooms Hotel Bookings
🔲 asiarooms.com

China Trip Hotel Bookings
🔲 english.ctrip.com
Chungking Mansions
🔲 chungking-mansions.hk
Hong Kong Hotels Association
🔲 hkha.org
YMCA
🔲 ymcahk.org.hk
Youth Hostel Association China
🔲 yhachina.com
Youth Hostel Association Hong Kong
🔲 yha.org.hk

Places to Stay

PRICE CATEGORIES
For a standard, double room per night (with breakfast if included), taxes and extra charges.
....
$ under HK$1,000 $$ HK$1,000–2,500 $$$ over HK$2,500

Super Luxury Hotels

The Langham
MAP M4 ■ 8 Peking Road, Tsim Sha Tsui, Kowloon ■ 2375 1133 ■ www.langhamhotels.com ■ $$
Restrained opulence reigns throughout. There's a good gym, pool and sauna, and many top-quality restaurants, including the impressive two-Michelin-starred T'ang Court, which is decked out like a Mongolian tent.

The Grand Hyatt
MAP N5 ■ 1 Harbour Rd, Wan Chai ■ 2588 1234 ■ www.hongkong.grand.hyatt.com ■ $$$
Next to the Convention Centre and the premier choice for unbridled luxury in Wan Chai, the Grand Hyatt has looked after world-famous guests including former US President Bill Clinton. Rooms have a modern feel, and include all the high-tech mod-cons.

Hotel InterContinental Hong Kong
MAP N4 ■ 18 Salisbury Rd, Kowloon ■ 2721 1211 ■ www.hongkong-ic. intercontinental.com ■ $$$
Popular with the rich and famous, the splendid, modern InterContinental is consistently voted among Asia's best hotels.

Two-thirds of the huge, beautifully appointed rooms offer fantastic harbour views.

Island Shangri-La
MAP M6 ■ Pacific Place, Central ■ 2877 3838 ■ www.shangri-la.com ■ $$$
The grandiose lobby, huge chandeliers and stunning mural adorning the atrium are a prelude to the elegantly decorated rooms, with terrific Peak or harbour views.

The Landmark Mandarin Oriental
MAP L5 ■ 15 Queen's Rd Central ■ 2132 0188 ■ www.mandarinoriental.com ■ $$$
A stylish conversion of former offices has created some of the largest rooms in Asia, all with circular sunken baths, HD TVs and Wi-Fi. The two-floor luxury spa is one of the city's best.

The Mandarin Oriental HK
MAP K4 ■ 5 Connaught Rd, Central ■ 2522 0111 ■ www.mandarinoriental.com ■ $$$
In an excellent location in the heart of the financial district, this fashionable hotel overlooks Victoria Harbour. The bustling public areas are one of the territory's most popular meeting places, while the rooms have an elegant atmosphere

and a modern, luxurious design, which incorporates every conceivable high-tech convenience.

The Peninsula
MAP N4 ■ Salisbury Rd, Kowloon ■ 2920 2888 ■ www.peninsula.com ■ $$$
Hong Kong's original luxury offering opened in 1928 and is still one of the city's best-loved hotels. Overlooking Victoria Harbour, the Neo-Classical Peninsula is famous for restrained luxury and excellent, friendly service (see p85).

The Venetian
Estrada da Baía de N Senhora da Esperança, Taipa, Macau ■ 2882 8888 ■ www.venetianmacao.com ■ $$$
Macau's most spectacular resort-casino is a recreation of the Las Vegas dream of Italy, but with sampans among the gondolas. The mega-resort is suites only, and has a themed shopping mall designed to look like the canals of Venice, a 1,800-seat theatre and all the dining options you could want.

Luxury Hotels

The Excelsior
MAP Q5 ■ 281 Gloucester Rd, Causeway Bay ■ 2894 8888 ■ www.excelsior hongkong.com ■ $$
The smart, modern and friendly Excelsior offers pretty much every in-room and hotel facility imaginable, as you'd expect from the Mandarin Oriental's sister.

Garden Hotel Guangzhou

368 Huangshi Dong Lu, Guangzhou ▪ 8333 8989 ▪ ww2.gardenhotel.com ▪ $$

The cavernous lobby gives a sense of the size of this imposing 1,000-plus room five-star hotel, boasting its own up-market shopping mall and good eating and drinking options. Weekend rates can be much lower.

Ritz-Carlton, Guangzhou

MAP L2 ▪ 3 Xing An Rd, Guangzhou ▪ 3813 6688 ▪ www.ritzcarlton.com ▪ $$

One of the city's finest luxury hotels is located in Pearl River City opposite the soaring Guangzhou Tower. Superlative luxury, superb amenities and classic Ritz-Carlton service.

Shangri-La Hotel Shenzhen

MAP D1 ▪ Jianshe Lu, Shenzhen ▪ 8233 0888 ▪ www.shangri-la.com ▪ $$

Close to the main shopping areas and railway station, the Shangri-la makes a great escape from Shenzhen's seething retail madness. The rooftop pool is perfect for relaxing.

Banyan Tree Macau

Galaxy Macau Resort, Avenida Marginal Flor de Lotus, Cotai Strip ▪ 8883 6688 ▪ www.banyantree.com/en/macau ▪ $$$

With great views of Macau's skyline, this magnificent resort hotel is supremely luxurious style and amenities. The award-winning rants and the ian-themed spa highest quality.

Hullett House

MAP M4 ▪ 2A Canton Rd, Tsim Sha Tsui ▪ 3988 0000 ▪ www.hulletthouse.com ▪ $$$

The blend of superb colonial architecture and contemporary interiors make this Hong Kong's top boutique hotel. Located in the beautiful former headquarters of the Marine Police, there are ten exquisitely designed suites with superb facilities as well as a fabulous stone terrace overlooking the Heritage 1881 courtyard.

Ritz-Carlton, Hong Kong

MAP L2 ▪ International Commerce Centre, 1 Austin Rd West, Kowloon ▪ 2263 2263 ▪ www.ritzcarlton.com ▪ $$$

The views are incredible from Hong Kong's tallest building. The quality of design and in-room technology make it the epitome of modern luxury. It also features the "highest bar in the world".

The Upper House

MAP M4 ▪ Pacific Place, 88 Queensway, Central ▪ 2918 1838 ▪ www.upperhouse.com ▪ $$$

This hotel has beautifully styled rooms with superb views and great facilities. Café Gray Deluxe restaurant and lounge on the 49th floor is a regular watering hole for Hong Kong's fashionable set.

Mid-Range Hotels in Hong Kong

The Eaton Hotel

MAP N1 ▪ 380 Nathan Rd ▪ 2782 1818 ▪ www.eaton-hotel.com ▪ $$

The best option in the Yau Ma Tei/Jordan area.

Rooms are smart and the lobby offers a flood of natural light, outdoor seating and an oasis of greenery.

Empire Hotel Kowloon

MAP N3 ▪ 62 Kimberley Road, Tsim Sha Tsui ▪ 3692 2222 ▪ www.empirehotel.com.hk ▪ $$

This very smart hotel with a modern gym and a lovely atrium pool is a complete contrast to its threadbare sister in Wan Chai. Rooms are equipped with the latest internet and audiovisual gadgetry. The location is perfect for Tsim Sha Tsui shopping and dining.

Hyatt Regency

MAP N4 ▪ 18 Hanoi Rd, Tsim Sha Tsui ▪ 2311 1234 ▪ hongkong.tsimshatsui.hyatt.com ▪ $$

Located in one of Kowloon's tallest towers, this impressive hotel is aimed at both business and leisure travellers. Rooms on the upper floors boast exceptional views out over Hong Kong and the hotel provides a great location for all the attractions on offer around Kowloon.

The Luxe Manor

MAP N3 ▪ 39 Kimberley Rd, Tsim Sha Tsui ▪ 3763 8888 ▪ www.theluxemanor.com ▪ $$

This stylish Kowloon boutique hotel combines eclectic, almost surreal, decor with high-tech features. The rooms are decorated with painted picture frames, which climb the walls onto the ceiling and other funky touches.

The Mira
MAP N3 ▪ 118 Nathan Rd, Tsim Sha Tsui ▪ 2368 1111 ▪ www.themira hotel.com ▪ $$
Chic, slick, futuristic and maybe lacking a little soul; however you cannot help admiring the redesign of this well-maintained business hotel. The infinity-edge pool and luxury spa are definite attractions.

Regal Airport Hotel
MAP B5 ▪ 9 Cheong Tat Rd, Chek Lap Kok ▪ 2286 8888 ▪ www.regalhotel. com ▪ $$
Hong Kong's largest hotel links directly to the airport terminal and features large rooms with avant-garde interior designs. Seven restaurants and bars provide a plethora of cuisine choices.

The Wesley
MAP N6 ▪ 22 Hennessy Rd, Wan Chai ▪ 2866 6688 ▪ www.ozohotels.com ▪ $$
Comfortable beds in modern rooms with city views and a central location make this a good choice on the island. Also has a small gym and high tech check-in and information screens in the lobby.

Mid-Range Hotels in Macau & China

Crowne Plaza Hotel and Suites Landmark, Shenzhen
3018 Nanhu Lu, Shenzhen ▪ 8217 2288 ▪ www.ihg.com ▪ $
Close to the railway station, this hotel offers lovely rooms and extensive facilities, including a health club, a gym and indoor pool.

Guangdong Victory Hotel
53 Shamian Bei Jie, Guangzhou ▪ 8121 6688 ▪ www.vhotel.com ▪ $
Formerly the Victoria Hotel, this hotel occupies two sites on Shamian Island – the main Neo-Classical block and the original colonial building. Facilities include several restaurants, a swimming pool and a sauna.

Best Western Shenzhen Felicity Hotel
1085 Heping Lu, Shenzhen ▪ 2558 6333 ▪ www.bwsz.net ▪ $$
This good-value hotel is reasonably well located and even boasts its own art gallery. Standards are high and guests can take advantage of the four restaurants as well as the gym, pool and sauna. Online bookings cost less than half the normal rate.

Holiday Inn
82–86 Rua de Pequim, Macau ▪ 2878 3333 ▪ www.holidayinn.com ▪ $$
Close by Lisboa's many casinos and convenient for the centre of Macau. Rooms (with cable TV) are blandly furnished but there's a good range of facilities, including gym, pool, sauna and a decent restaurant for Cantonese and Szechuan food.

Hotel Royal Macau
Estrada da Vitoria 2–4, Macau ▪ 2855 2222 ▪ www.hotelroyal.com. mo ▪ $$
The Hotel Royal is one of Macau's oldest hotels and it shows. That said, it is clean and well run, although the rooms offer

little more than the basics. It has an indoor pool, gym (with some ageing equipment) and sauna. It's also close to the heart of town and within sight of the pretty Guia Lighthouse.

Ole Tai Sam Un Hotel
43–45 Rua da Caldeira, Macau ▪ 2893 8818 ▪ oletaisamunhotel.com ▪ $$
Located close to Macau's historic centre, this hotel offers well-equipped, modern rooms with hardwood floors and tasteful decor. The breakfast buffet includes a good variety of options. Senado Square is a 10 minute walk away.

The Panglin Hotel
2002 Jiabin Lu, Lowu, Shenzhen ▪ 2518 5888 ▪ www.panglin-hotel. com ▪ $$
Smart and modern, this is one of Shenzhen's superior hotels, about 4 km (2 miles) from the railway station. Room sizes are decent and all come with cable TV. Services include station shuttle bus, babysitting and 24-hour room service. Numerous dining options; Sky Paradise buffet on the 50th floor is Shenzhen's highest revolving restaurant.

Value-for-Money Hotels

2 Macdonnell Road
MAP K6 ▪ 2 Macdonnell Rd, Central ▪ 2132 2132 ▪ www.twomr.com.hk ▪
With pleasant rooms, good Central location excellent views acr the Zoological an

Botanical Gardens to the city and harbour, Macdonnell Road offers good value apartments. Maid service, free local calls, use of gym, satellite and cable TV, kitchenette and Central shuttle bus are all included in the price. Long-stay packages also available.

BP International House
MAP M2 ■ 8 Austin Rd, Tsim Sha Tsui ■ 2376 1111 ■ www.bpih.com.hk ■ $$
The boxy rooms with ugly 1980s wallpaper have smallish beds, but the place is clean, efficient and can be cheap, and has lovely views over Kowloon Park.

The Empire Hotel
MAP N6 ■ 33 Hennessy Rd, Wan Chai ■ 3692 2111 ■ www.empirehotel. com.hk ■ $$
Marooned between the area's two main roads, the Empire is right in the heart of Wan Chai so you're paying for location rather than luxury, as the cheap fittings will constantly remind you. Still, the prices are competitive, the service isn't bad and there's a rooftop pool, plus a gym and free broadband internet access.

The Harbourview
MAP N5 ■ 4 Harbour Rd, Wan Chai ■ 2911 1358 ■ theharbourview.com.hk ■ $$
This modest Chinese YMCA-run hotel charges a premium for the location, but low-season discounts are available. Rooms are comfortable and well-appointed. Two restaurants and a gym.

Rosedale on the Park
MAP Q6 ■ 8 Shelter St, Causeway Bay ■ 2127 8888 ■ hongkong. rosedalehotels.com ■ $$
This self-styled "cyber boutique hotel" offers reasonable value overlooking Victoria Park. The look is sleek and modern. The rooms are small but well laid-out and there is a range of business services.

The Salisbury YMCA
MAP M4 ■ 41 Salisbury Rd, Tsim Sha Tsui ■ 2268 7000 ■ www.ymcahk.org. hk ■ $$
Don't be put off by the initials. For value, views and location, the always-popular YMCA, next door to the posh Peninsula, can't be beaten. The well-furnished rooms are spacious, equipped with laptop ports, and satellite and cable TV. A swimming pool, sauna, gym and an indoor climbing wall round off the facilities. Family suites are terrific.

Shamrock
MAP N4 ■ 223 Nathan Rd ■ 2735 2271 ■ www.sham rockhotel.com.hk ■ $$
The rather severe lobby opens onto Nathan Road, and the dishevelled lifts lead up to big rooms with satellite TV and air conditioning, and it has a business centre.

The Wharney
MAP N6 ■ 57–73 Lockhart Rd, Wan Chai ■ 2861 1000 ■ www.wharney.com ■ $$
Right in the increasingly smart centre of Wan Chai, the Wharney offers

decent surroundings, a revamped gym and pool, sauna, business centre and a couple of restaurants. Rooms are well-appointed but a bit small.

Cheap Sleeps

Bradbury Hall Hostel
MAP F3 ■ Chek Keng, Sai Kung, New Territories ■ 2328 2458 ■ www. yha.org.hk ■ $
As you might expect from its remote location, this hostel has basic, barrack-like dorms. Those with tents may want to walk on and pitch camp at Tai Long Wan's lovely beaches nearby.

Bradbury Jockey Club Youth Hostel
MAP F2 ■ 66 Tai Mei Tuk, New Territories ■ 2662 5123 ■ www.yha.org.hk ■ $
This very pleasant hostel by the reservoir makes for a good base or stop-off for walkers exploring the beautiful Plover Cove area. Air-conditioned singles, doubles or dorms are available.

Caritas Bianchi Lodge
MAP N1 ■ 4 Cliff Rd, Yau Ma Tei, Kowloon ■ 2388 1111 ■ www. caritas-chs.org.hk ■ $
Like Booth Lodge next door, there's only a chapel and restaurant-cum-café to amuse you here. Still, the rooms are large by any standards. The hotel is run by the Social Welfare Bureau of the Roman Catholic Church.

For a key to hotel price categories see p148

Chungking House, Chungking Mansions

MAP N4 ■ Block 4A/5F, 40 Nathan Rd, Tsim Sha Tsui ■ 2739 1600 ■ www. chungkinghouse.com ■ $

Staying at the mansions is a badge of honour to some budget travellers, an unpleasant necessity to others (see p87). The dingy hallways lead to dozens of guesthouses offering cheap accommodation in an excellent location. Oppressive but fascinating, this is Hong Kong's cultural melting pot. Chungking House is probably the best option, with larger rooms than most.

Holy Carpenter Guest House

MAP R2 ■ 1 Dyer Ave, Hung Hom, Kowloon ■ 2362 0301 ■ www. holycarpenter.org/ holyHotel/index.htm ■ $

Run by the Sheng Kung Hui Holy Carpenter Church, this is a pleasant alternative to the dingier guesthouse offerings in Chungking and Mirador, but stuck out in boring old Hung Hom. Facilities in double and triple rooms are basic but include TV, phone, bathroom, shower and air conditioning.

Sze Lok Yuen Hostel

MAP D3 ■ Tai Mo Shan, Tseun Wan, New Territories ■ 2488 8188 ■ www.yha.org.hk ■ $

A very basic hikers' crash-pad, Sze Lok Yuen is close to the summit of Tai Mo Shan, Hong Kong's tallest peak. The views of the surrounding mountains are spectacular, but its dorm rooms are pretty basic with no fans or air conditioning. The altitude cools things down though

in all but the hottest months. Camping is also permitted here.

YHA Mei Ho House Youth Hostel

MAP M1 ■ Block 41, Shek Kip Mei Estate, Sham Shui Po, Kowloon ■ 3728 3500 ■ www.yha.org.hk ■ $

A fully renovated public resettlement block from 1954, this hostel has en-suite air-conditioned doubles, family rooms and dorms. There is an on-site store, café, shared kitchen and laundry.

Booth Lodge

MAP N1 ■ 11 Wing Sing Lane, Yau Ma Tei, Kowloon ■ 2771 9266 ■ www. salvationarmy.org.hk/en/ services/booth ■ $$

Air-conditioned rooms with a shower, bath, fridge, phone and TV are merely adequate, but the location and prices are great at this Salvation Army-run hotel.

Long-Stay Hotels

The Bay Bridge

MAP D3 ■ 123 Castle Peak Rd, Yau Kom Tau, Tsuen Wan, Kowloon ■ 2945 1111 ■ www.baybridgehong kong.com ■ HK$17,100–$28,000 per month

Given the Tseun Wan location, these smart studio and suite apart-ments are not for those who must be at the centre of things. Facilities include a gym and outdoor pool.

Chi Residences

MAP J4 ■ 138 Connaught Rd West, Sai Ying Pun ■ 3443 6888 ■ www.chi-residences.com ■ from HK$35,800 per month

The beautifully appointed rooms here are decorated in a contemporary style

and have views of Victoria Harbour. Chi Residences manage several properties in other locations in Hong Kong.

J Plus Boutique Hotel

MAP Q6 ■ 1–5 Irving St, Causeway Bay ■ 3196 9000 ■ www.jplushong kong.com ■ HK$42,000–$68,000 per month

Hong Kong's first boutique hotel, the interior was originally by the French designer Philippe Starck and has since been revamped by his protégés. The studios and one-room suites are the perfect blend of comfort and luxury and come equipped with kitchens and washing machines.

Ovolo Sheung Wan

MAP J5 ■ 222 Hollywood Rd, Sheung Wan ■ 2165 1000 ■ www.ovolohotels. com ■ HK$35,000 per month

These swanky modern residences are well-located close to the heart of Central. They have all the facilities of a deluxe hotel, including kitchen-ettes, free super-fast Wi-Fi, Apple TV and in-room washing machine and tumble dryer.

Shama Central

MAP K5 ■ 26 Peel St, Central ■ MAP K5 ■ 2103 1713 ■ www.shama.com ■ HK$33,000–$77,800 per month

Centrally located above a bustling produce market, this modern block offers cosy studios and spacious apartments with smart furnishings, daily maid service, Wi-Fi internet access, self-service laundry and a gym.

Yes Inn

MAP E4 ■ 4/F, 10 Anchor St, Tai Kok Tsui, Kowloon ■ 3427 6000 ■ www. yesinn.com ■ HK$9,500–$18,000 per month
Bright, small and inexpensive serviced apartments in a residential area. The cheaper options have TV and complimentary Wi-Fi, but no kitchenette.

Great Escapes

Hong Kong Gold Coast Hotel

MAP B3 ■ 1 Castle Peak Rd, Kowloon ■ 2452 8888 ■ www.sino-hotels.com ■ $
This 10-hectare (24-acre) resort offers sea views from its well-equipped rooms. The accommodation complex is unlovely from outside, but recreation facilities include pool, pitch-and-putt golf course, tennis courts and running track.

Jockey Club Mount Davis Youth Hostel

MAP E5 ■ Mount Davis Path, Kennedy Town ■ 2817 5715 ■ www. yha.org.hk ■ $
Popular budget option for the more adventurous, this lovely and friendly hostel sits atop Mount Davis at the western edge of Hong Kong Island. The surroundings are peaceful and beautiful, and the staff are helpful. A little out of the way so you may need to take a taxi there.

Pousada de Coloane

Praia de Cheoc-Van, Coloane Island, Macau ■ 2888 2143 ■ www.hotel pcoloane.com.mo ■ $
This tiny, remote hotel lies at the far end of Coloane, overlooking a small, pretty beach. It boasts a nice swimming pool, deck area and an attractive Portuguese-style restaurant and bar. Room fittings are showing their age, but are well equipped.

San Va

65–67 Rua da Felicidade, Macau ■ www.sanvahotel. com ■ No credit cards ■ $
Step back in time with this genuine 1920s guesthouse. Rooms have ceiling fans and wash basin, and all other facilities are shared. San Va is clean, romantic and lovingly run.

Grand Coloane Resort

Estrada de Hac Sa 1918, Ilha de Coloane, Macau ■ 2887 1111 ■ www. grandcoloane.com ■ $$
All rooms come with their own terrace and sea views. There's a small sandy beach and an 18-hole golf course. You can also practise your swing on the ocean driving range with balls that float.

Harbour Plaza Resort City

MAP C2 ■ 18 Tin Yan Rd, Tin Shui Wai, New Territories ■ 2180 6688 ■ www.harbour-plaza. com ■ $$
Out in the New Territories, this extensive resort complex offers a vast array of sports and recreation facilities, including cinemas, shops, gyms, sports tracks and courts, Chinese and international restaurants, and nearby historical and beauty spots. All rooms include the basics with a small lounge area.

The Warwick

MAP C6 ■ East Bay, Cheung Chau ■ 2981 0081 ■ $$
A cheap alternative to city living, magical Cheung Chau's only major hotel offers fine sea views next to good beaches with windsurf and kayak hire. Great coastal walks are around the headland. Furnishings are nothing special, and the exterior is 1960s municipal.

White Swan Hotel

1 Southern St, Shamian Island, Guangzhou ■ 8188 6968 ■ www. whiteswanhotel.com ■ $$
Overlooking the Pearl River on sleepy Shamian Island, this opulent hotel is the place to relax in Guangzhou.

Pousada de São Tiago

Avenida de República, Fortaleza de São Tiago de Barra, Macau ■ 2837 8111 ■ www.saotiago.com.mo ■ $$$
Converted from an old Portuguese fort hewn from the rock in the 17th century, this tiny hotel looking across the bay to mainland China is a picturesque delight. The comfortable, Portuguese-style rooms are heavily but beautifully decorated.

Tai O Heritage Hotel

MAP A5 ■ Shek Tsai Po Street, Tai O, Lantau Island ■ 2985 8383 ■ $$$
Housed in an 110-year-old former colonial police station, this beautiful hotel is the perfect base from which to explore the sleepy fishing town on Tai O and Lantau Island beyond. The five rooms and four suites are all individually decorated in an elegant, colonial style.

For a key to hotel price categories see p148

Index

Acknowledgments

Author
Liam Fitzpatrick, Jason Gagliardi, Andrew Stone

Additional contributor
David Leffman

Publishing Director Georgina Dee

Publisher Vivien Antwi

Design Director Phil Ormerod

Editorial Michelle Crane, Rachel Fox, Freddie Marriage, Alison McGill, Fíodhna Ní Ghríofa, Scarlett O'Hara, Sally Schafer, Beverly Smart, Hollie Teague, Vinita Venugopal

Design Richard Czapnik, Sunita Gahir, Bharti Karakoti, Marisa Renzullo, Jaynan Spengler

Commissioned Photography Nigel Hicks, David McIntyre, Rough Guides/Tim Draper, Rough Guides/Karen Trist, Chris Stowers

Picture Research Susie Peachey, Ellen Root, Lucy Sienkowska, Oran Tarjan

Cartography Jasneet Arora, Suresh Kumar, James Macdonald
Cartography derived from Bartholomew Digital Database

DTP Jason Little, George Nimmo

Production Linda Dare

Factchecker Charles Young

Proofreader Ruth Reisenberger

Indexer Kathryn O'Donoghue

Illustrator Lee Redmond

Blue Island Publishing, London

Picture Credits
The publisher would like to thank the following for their kind permission to reproduce their photographs:
(Key: a-above; b-below/bottom; c-centre; f-far; l-left; r-right; t-top)

123RF.com: danielvfung 19tl; Fedor Selivanov 10b.

4Corners: Claudio Cassaro 1, 2tl, 8–9, 24–5; Guido Cozzi 4b; Günter Gräfenhain 3tl, 62–3; Huw Jones 4cr; Luigi Vaccarella 4crb.

Alamy Images: Agencja Fotograficzna Caro 10cl; Asia Photopress 66b; Andrew Barnes 13clb; Carlo Bollo 59tl; Andrew Cawley 7tl, 58b; Pak Hung Chan 51tr; Pavlos Christoforou 50br; Charles Crust 93t; Flirt 60bc; Foto 28 95bl; FPLA 109cla; Glyn Genin 124bc; Hemis 55tl, 135t; Hemis/Degas Jeanne-Pierre 80tr; John Henshall 68c; imageBROKER/Ingo Schulz 11cla; ImageRite 45tr; Islandspics HK 31bl; JoeFoxBerlin 16bl; JTB Media Creation 84cla; Moon Yin Lam 121cla; Andrew Linscott 108cla; Jon Lord 47tl; Arnel Manalang 32clb; Stefano Politi Markovina 103bl; Hilke Maunder 46t; Kees Metselaar 32br; My Favourite Lens 23bl; Prisma Bildagentur AG/Vidler Steve 83clb, 108b; Radharc Images/Joe Fox 64tl; Radharc Images/Joe Fox 72tr, 97tr; Robert Harding Picture Library/Ian Trower 31tl; RosalreneBetancourt 6 11cra; Paul Rushton 43b; Peter Scholey 47br; Jose Luis Stephens 23tl; Tao Images Ltd/Songhui Huang 131cra; Travel Pictures 73t; Ian Trower 19br; Vinicius Valle 96br; Ron Yue 43cl.

Amaroni's Little Italy: 105br.

Casa Sai Kung: 113cr.

Castelo Concepts: 114tl.

Corbis: Bettmann 36b; Massimo Borchi 94tr; Dallas and John Heaton 2tr, 34–5; Destinations 59br; Victor Fraile 136bl; Robert Harding World Imagery/Gavin Hellier 41bl; James Marshall 67bc; Wally McNamee 37br; Redlink/Lo Mak 117br; Ian Trower 131br; 145/ Ocean/Wilfred Y Wong 51cl; xPACIFICA 38clb.

Dreamstime.com: Steve Allen 124tl; Au_yeung225 48tl; Bjeayes 80cl; Evgenia Bolyukh 29tl; Olteanu Calin 123br; Cheechew 120bl; Acon Cheng 125bl; Earnesttse 42t; Eddiekwokcf 14cb; Efired 4cla; Galinasavina 33clb; Dejia Gao 134cr; Jorg Hackemann 68tl; Hannamariah 137tr; Xin Hua 89tl; Hupeng 48c; Jingaiping 94bl, 100cla; Mike K. 76tl; Kewuwu 67tl; Kiankhoon 45bl; Stanislav Komogorov 79cra; Sergii Koval 57cla; Kwokfai 86bl; Nohead Lam 16–17; Lance Lee 126tl; Yiu Tung Lee 22–3, 44bl, 45cla, 106tl; Keng Po Leung 39, 40tc, 81tl; Logray 87bl; Mooindy 96tr; Roland Nagy 10tr; Matee Nuserm 136bl; Ohmaymay 50tl; Leung Cho Pan 6cl, 101tr; Patrickmak039 86t; Paulwongwan 117tr; Sean Pavone 3tr, 49tl, 65tr, 138–9b; William Perry 21tl, 92tl; Pindiyath100 11tr, 32–3, 39cr; 48bc, 50c, 76br, 78tr, 82tr, 88br; 89cr,104cra,104bl, 112cra; Pixattitude 16cl, 61cl, 74t, 101br; Plotnikov 14cla; Poupaep 4t; Saiko3p 39tl, 102t; Nick Kee Son 98–9; Stbernardstudio 12cl; StrippedPixel 30–31, 107br; Szefei 56cl; Torsakarin 56br; Wing Ho Tsang 49cra, 88cla; Thor Jorgen Udvang 6tr; Jeremy Wee 33tl; Ho Nam Wong 111br; Xishuiyuan 132b; Yourlettertome 105ca; Jess Yu 11crb, 28–9, 41tr, 118b, 123tr; Lai Ching Yuen 44tc; Ziggymars 122tl; Zkruger 22clb, 80b.

Drop: 53t.

Fernando's: 129br.

Four Seasons Hotel Hong Kong: 54clb,

Getty Images: AFP/Mike Clarke15crb;
Philippe Lopez 68br; Doug Armand 56tl
Clarke 81clb; Victor Fraile 61tr; Universa
History Archive 36cb; Stefan Irvine 12br;
jalvaran 75bl; John Hudson Photography
Ross Kinnaird 132tr; Loic Lagarde 11br;
Lakatos 37cla; Lonely Planet Images 21
Maremagnum 112bl; Thomas Reucker 7
rexlam 119cla; Lars Ruecker 57tr; Haral
Sund 60t; Pawel Toczynski 14–15.

Grand Lisboa: 127bl.

Hong Kong Heritage Museum: 26clb, 26
26–7, 27cra, 27br.

Hongkong Land Limited: www.dadokit.co
69t.

Hotel InterContinental, Hong Kong: 90t, 9

Island Shangri-La: 77cl.

Mandarin Oriental, Macau: 128t.

One Thirty-One: 115br.

Ritz-Carlton, Hong Kong: 52b.

Robert Harding Picture Library: Amanda
Hall 4cl; Mel Longhurst 33cb; Fumio Okad
18–19; David Sellwood 118cra; Ian Trower
4clb, 20–21.

**Shangri-La International Hotel Manageme.
Limited:** 133tr.

SuperStock: Juzant 23crb; Iain Masterton
17tr; Steve Vidler 20cl.

The Hong Kong Jockey Club: 17bl.

The Landmark Mandarin Oriental: 70t.

The Peninsula Hotel Limited Hong Kong:
55c, 55b.

The Venetian Macao: Visual Media 127cra.

Cover

Front and spine – Dreamstime.com:
Noppakun

Back – Dreamstime.com: Poupaep t.

Pull Out Map Cover

Dreamstime.com: Noppakun

All other images © Dorling Kindersley

For further information see:
www.dkimages.com

*As a guide to abbreviations in visitor information
blocks:* **Adm** = admission charge.